Friendly Family:
A Parent's Guide for Nurturing Positive Sibling Relationships

by Linda Clark

Formatted, Converted, and Distributed by eBookIt.com
http://www.eBookIt.com

ISBN-13: 9781456641627 (paperback)
ISBN-13: 9781456641610 (ebook)
ISBN-13: 9781456641634 (audiobook)

Dear Esteemed Reader,

Thank you immensely for choosing this book to join your collection. We imagine that you've already embarked on an exploration of ideas within these pages, and we couldn't be happier about it!

Now, if you find yourself chuckling, pondering, or even debating with the words in front of you, we'd absolutely love to hear about it. If you can spare a few moments to pen down your thoughts in a review, we would be as delighted as a dictionary on a spelling bee!

An Amazon review would be excellent - but hey, we're far from picky. Whether it's a scribble on the back of a grocery list, a tweet, or even a message in a bottle (though that might take a while to reach us), your feedback is gold.

Writing a review might not be as fun as a spontaneous dance-off, but we promise it'll bring grins to our faces, warmth to our hearts, and incredibly valuable insights to future readers.

With Gratitude,

Bo Bennett, PhD
Publisher
Archieboy Holdings, LLC.

Contents

Introduction

Welcome to a comprehensive guide that is targeted at paving the way for healthier relationships between your children. Many parents find themselves longing to cultivate a bond between siblings that transcends the typical rivalries of early years, hoping to shape a lifelong friendship. This book provides a practical roadmap and useful insights into fostering these vital relationships beginning from the earliest interaction and evolving well into adulthood. By combining the benefits of in-depth psychology, proven strategies, and real-life experiences, it's intended this guide serves as a valuable resource throughout your parenting journey. The aim is not merely to manage sibling rivalries, but to set the stage for a powerful, lifelong bond between your children, by laying the groundwork from day one and guiding them in their unique paths. Through it all, you'll foster incredible individuality within family unity, paving the way for a harmonious home, resilient bonds, and navigating modern-day challenges. No stone is left unturned, so let's embark on this enlightening journey into the world of siblinghood together.

The Power of Sibling Bonds

If we're talking about lifelong relationships, let's acknowledge one of the longest relationships that most people will ever have—a relationship with their sibling(s). The sibling bond is often the first peer relationship a child experiences. It's a unique interchange encompassing shared experiences, genetics, and often a shared environment. This bond leaves an indelible mark on the personalities, behaviors, and lives of our children.

Sibling bonds vary naturally, and these differences aren't necessarily a bad thing. In some sibling dynamics, companionship shines through from day one, creating a natural flow leading to a lifelong connection. For others, the bond may take time and patience to cultivate. It's all part of the journey. Every disagreement, every laugh shared, every tear shed, strengthens this bond in its unique way.

It's this bond that can help our kids cross the bridge of adversities. Having a sibling can be like having a built-in best friend, someone to lean onto when life gets tough. The friendly hand of a sibling can provide comfort, understanding, and help in navigating the curves of life.

Your role as a parent in tending to your children's relationships with one another is multi-layered. The care you show to each child, the model you set on how to resolve conflict, and the values you instill all go a long way to strengthen their bonds. We should remember that as parents, we're not just raising individuals, we're nurturing a sibling group—a unit within a unit.

While the parental role isn't to handhold through every conflict, it's essential to guide your children in learning appropriate conflict resolution and respect for differences. We can't guarantee the road to adulthood will be smooth, but we can ensure they are equipped with teamwork skills, empathy, and respect, instilled during their earliest years.

Importantly, sibling bonds shouldn't overshadow the necessity of individuality. Each child should feel respected and loved for who they are individually. They should be allowed the freedom to discover their own paths, interests, and dreams. Their individual identities strengthen the family as much as their shared experiences and collective sibling identity do.

It's worth noting that the strength of sibling bonds doesn't always stem from consistency and harmony. It's often the storms weathered together that builds resiliency, and that resiliency not only strengthens their bond but also equips them with survival mechanisms to face the world individually.

Infusing fun family traditions and activities can also enhance sibling bonds. Shared experiences, whether it's a weekend movie night or a summer camping trip, can create fond memories and strengthen their connection. While it's crucial to respect individual interests, forging time for shared enjoyment goes a long way in nurturing sibling bonds over the years.

As siblings age, paths may diverge. New relationships may evolve, careers might separate them geographically, or just the bustle of adult life might distance them. Nevertheless, the seeds of affinity sown during childhood can help sustain that strong bond. As parents, fostering open communication, instilling the importance of family, and encouraging shared memories could serve as the glue that binds them.

Keep in mind that sibling relationships are complex and evolve over time. It is perfectly normal for these relationships to shift through various stages of closeness and distance. Be patient and supportive throughout these changes and avoid forcing a certain type of relationship onto your children. Their bond is their own unique journey.

Let's remember that as much as you, as parents, play a role in influencing your children's bond, it's equally important to let it naturally flourish. Nurture their relationship with love, respect, and patience. What you want to instill is a sense that, regardless of life's twists and turns, the sibling bond is consistent and dependable, lending a steady hand in both times of happiness and adversity.

With that understanding, the goal is to establish a familial environment where each child feels valued, heard, and loved. Where their differences are appreciated as strengths rather than drawbacks. This enriches not only the individual well-being of each child but also the lifelong bond they share as siblings.

It's not an easy task, and the dynamics will vary from family to family, but the time, effort, and love invested pay off exponentially. The sibling bond is one of the most enduring they'll share throughout their lives, standing as a source of support, love, shared memories, and deep understanding. It's truly a bond like no other.

By prioritizing this aspect of your children's relationship, we're fostering a heartfelt, time-tested connection that will endure through each phase of life, beyond the confines of childhood, into their adult years and beyond. This is the power of the sibling bond, the impact of which transcends years and life circumstances.

Setting the Stage for Lifelong Friendships

Having laid out the unique power of sibling relationships in previous chapters, it's now time to dive deeper into how we, as parents, can cultivate an environment and family culture conducive to building those close, lifelong friendships between our children.

These sibling relationships are an essential part of family-life that mold our offspring's growth and development. It's the friendship they don't choose but come to appreciate with time that teaches them the profound essence of kinship and mutual understanding.

Are the dynamics always smooth? No. But don't fret. There will be hiccups, rivalries, and disagreements, but these too can be instrumental in shaping their values, their ability to navigate relationships and handle conflict.

Let's begin by thinking about the foundation of these friendships. Fostering such bonds doesn't happen by accident. As parents, we need to stay proactive, creating an environment that encourages empathy, understanding, and mutual respect.

A critical first step in this process is encouraging and facilitating open communication. To sow the seeds of lifelong friendships, we have to help our children voice their feelings and thoughts, nurture an environment in which every voice is heard and seems respected, even during disagreements.

Exemplify good communication in your day-to-day interactions. Let them see you engaging in meaningful conversations, handling disputes appropriately, and listening actively. As they see and participate in this, they will carry these habits into their sibling relationships too.

Next, we must ensure to validate each child's unique identity. While it's easier to lump all the kids together, remember, they're individual beings with their own interests, inclinations, and aspirations. Respect and acknowledge these differences.

If one child loves reading, nurture that and recommend good books. If the other prefers sports, play ball. Show them it's not about comparison, but about mutual respect and appreciation of each other's strengths. That's how we pave the way for lifelong connections.

While acknowledging the individuality, encourage collaborations and shared goals between siblings. Joint projects give them a sense of camaraderie and joint ownership that can tighten their bond.

However, keep an eye out for any competitive dynamics that may brew during such activities. Ensure competition is healthy and not destructive, that it contributes to their relationship, and doesn't deter it.

Now, respect doesn't come naturally to kids. As parents, it's our responsibility to guide them towards it. How we treat them and how we let them treat us sets the foundation for these habits. Set boundaries and clear consequences for disrespect. Ultimately, they'll carry these taught norms into their sibling relationships.

Importantly, avoid favoritism. It's a poison pill that can undermine these precious bonds even before they fully cultivate. Treat each child with equal affection, attention, and discipline. Refrain from comparing them, as it can fuel a competitive streak, lead to resentment, and hamper potential friendships.

Lastly, offer them opportunities for bonding. Family trips, rituals, or simple things like a movie night or cooking together can work wonders. Shared memories and experiences become the thread that binds them together in the long run.

Remember, as parents, we're the architects of the family dynamics. We have the power to either create a nurturing environment that fosters lifelong friendships or let sibling rivalry run its course. Let's choose the former, for strong sibling connections are a legacy every parent would want to leave behind.

Through this section, we've provided a comprehensive plan for setting the stage for lifelong friendships among siblings.

It's now up to you, as guardians, to implement these suggestions, adapt them to your family's unique circumstances, and observe the delightful bonds that develop as a result.

Chapter 1:
The Nature of Siblinghood

With the stage set for the exploration of the power of sibling bonds, we now delve into the captivating realm of siblinghood and its essence. Sibling relationships, which are often marked by a unique mix of rivalry and revelry, have been a subject of fascination throughout history. This peculiar dynamic is not a modern phenomenon; history is replete with instances of sibling partnerships that changed the course of civilizations and sibling rivalries that led to catastrophic conflicts. Concurrently, psychological perspectives provide profound insights into the underpinnings of sibling bonds from the cradle to the grave. These bonds are influenced by diverse factors including familial environments, parenting styles, personal temperaments, and even birth order. The ties between siblings are capable of shaping individual identities while also constructing a shared family narrative. It's crucial to understand that the nature of siblinghood is multifaceted, complex, and incredibly impactful to each child's development journey. Yet, it's this intricate dance between rivalry and camaraderie, individual growth, and shared experiences that imbue sibling relationships with their monumental potential.

From Rivalry to Revelry: A Historical Perspective

As we dive into the historical perspective of sibling relationships, it's crucial to understand that sibling rivalries are not just a modern-day phenomenon. These dynamics have always been part of family makeup worldwide.

Throughout time and across cultures, sibling relationships have continually transformed as societal norms and familial constructions shifted. In ancient times, children were often seen in the context of their contributions to the family unit, their roles primarily rooted in chores and labor. As such, rivalries often stemmed from competition for resources or recognition within the family.

Move to the Middle Ages and the Renaissance, siblings were usually left to navigate their relationships without much adult intervention. Parents often had larger families and less time to focus on the individual relationships between their children.

Perspective towards sibling relationships started transforming significantly during the Industrial Revolution. As families moved from farms to cities and homes shrank in size, sibling dynamics became more intense, the rivalry was even more prevalent, and the idea of siblinghood as a significant aspect of childhood came to fore.

Consider 19th Century Victorian England, where large families became less common and parents started delivering more focused attention on their kids. This led to a shift to a bond-based approach in which parents sought to nurture closer emotional ties between their children.

Fast forward to the late 20th Century, we see the influence of advancements in psychology highlighting the formative effect of sibling interaction on a child's social and emotional development. This led to an increased focus on managing sibling rivalries and encouraging joyous relationships.

Let's take a moment to underscore the influence of the media. Think about shows like "The Brady Bunch" or "Full House." They shaped and reflected our perspectives of sibling relationships – showcasing both the rivalries and the strong bonds of love and camaraderie.

Enter the 21st Century and we see smaller families, with increased parent engagement, and a more conscious effort to foster harmony among siblings. Nevertheless, sibling rivalry remains a tricky and common part of family dynamics, even in this era of helicopter parenting and tiger mothers.

While history can't provide a how-to guide for managing sibling relationships, it reminds us that these relationships are complex and always evolving, shaped by familial contexts and societal changes. It's up to us, as parents, to continuously learn and adapt our approaches to guide our children towards strong, healthy bonds.

An understanding of historical perspectives also provides some factors that have consistently influenced sibling relationships, namely birth order, gender, individual temperament, and parental influence.

Historically, birth order has often determined roles and responsibilities within the family, which in turn affected sibling interactions. Gender, too, has held significant sway. For example, traditional societies often favored males, thereby fostering rivalries among brothers for inheritance or amongst sisters and brothers.

A child's individual temperament has always been a variable factor influencing these dynamics. Two children from the same family can have entirely different experiences because of their unique dispositions and how they individually interpret and react to situations.

Lastly, parental influence is a factor that has been under the radar but has always played a tremendous role in shaping sibling dynamics. Historical perspectives remind us that the way parents manage disagreements, show affection, or confer responsibilities significantly influences the texture of the relationship between siblings.

By understanding these historical underpinnings, we're better positioned to grasp why sibling rivalries develop and, more importantly, how they can be guided towards harmonious sibling relationships.

The goal isn't to eliminate rivalry, dismiss disputes or strive for an unrealistic idyllic relationship between siblings. Instead, it's about learning to navigate these choppy waters with empathy and understanding, steering towards a close bond that celebrates individual strengths, differences, and ultimately uncovers the revelry in the rivalry.

Psychological Perspectives on Sibling Bonds

Now that we've set the historical stage of sibling relationships, let's head into the world of psychology to better understand sibling bonds. By navigating through various psychological perspectives, we can further illuminate the inherent complexities of these crucial relationships.

The immense emotional influence siblings have on each other can be easily overlooked due to its commonplace nature. But from a psychological standpoint, the presence of siblings and the intricate dynamics they foster are a foundational building block in each child's overall development.

Primarily, it's important to remember that sibling relationships provide an arena where children can practice social skills. These interactions allow children to learn how to handle conflict, practice behavior inhibition, and develop empathy. Like a safe proving ground, children test various emotional responses, actions, and reactions in sibling-centered relationships.

From a psychoanalytic perspective, siblings invariably influence each other's identities and self-concepts. Whether consciously or subconsciously, children often define who they are based on how they differ from their siblings. The process of self-definition can get tricky though, especially when multiple children vie to establish their unique identities within a family.

As parents, understanding the psychological mechanisms shaping your children's interactions can aid in mediating conflicts and fostering positive relationships. For example, according to the Social Learning Theory, behaviors can be understood within their social context, meaning behaviors often are learned through modeling and reinforcement. With this in mind, it's critical to ensure our actions and behaviors set the best example for our children.

Similarly, the family systems perspective places emphasis on the interconnectedness of all family members. From this view, one's behavior influences and is influenced by the behaviors of others within the family system. Harmony within siblings may be achieved by understanding this complex web of relationships and addressing any imbalances.

Further, the Attachment Theory stresses the importance of forming secure bonds during childhood, which tend to form the basis of future relationships. In addition to the parent-child bond, sibling attachments are often significant sources of security and comfort for children, a reality that underscores the importance of nurturing these bonds.

It's also key to understand that a child's perspective on sibling relationships might differ from an adult's viewpoint. Bonding might be based on shared interests or activities, common friends, or even shared adversities. Fostering these common grounds can strengthen sibling relationships and encourage a supportive atmosphere.

It's also interesting to explore the Adlerian theory perspective, which highlights birth order and perceived parental favoritism's impact on sibling relationships. There's often an inherent competition among siblings influenced by these factors, causing siblings to act out or supress feelings to secure their place in the family hierarchy.

The myriad emotions siblings experience — ranging from intense love, fierce rivalry, deep resentment, and unconditional support — are all part of these unique bonds. These relationships, fraught with contradictions, are a natural ground for a child to explore a whole spectrum of emotions safely and organically.

As we delve into these psychological perspectives, it's essential to keep in mind that each family dynamic is unique, and there's no one-size-fits-all approach. Therefore, understanding multiple perspectives can provide a comprehensive toolset to address varied situations that may arise in your family.

Examining sibling relationships through a psychological lens isn't about labeling or diagnosing issues. Instead, it's about better understanding the underlying dynamics and using this knowledge to support your children. With awareness and compassion, you can guide your children in forging mutually respectful, understanding, and loving sibling bonds.

In the upcoming chapter, we'll extend on these psychological perspectives and provide tangible steps you can take right from the start to foster early bonds, starting from preparation for a new family member to mastering the crucial first interactions.

Chapter 2:
Laying the Groundwork from Day One

After understanding siblinghood's nature in the previous chapter, it's time to delve into the pivotal first steps for promoting healthy sibling relationships. From the moment you announce a new addition to the family, the groundwork for sibling relationships begins. Navigating this new dynamic will require careful planning and a good dose of patience. Yet, it's important to remember that, like any journey worth taking, laying the groundwork for lasting bonds from day one is a process full of unpredictability and joy. While the initial interactions between your children may not always go as you envisioned, they lay a crucial foundation for the richness of sibling relationships moving forward. The first reactions, initial adjustments and the ensuing bonds formed are important moments that set the tone for enduring sibling love and understanding. Nurturing this early bond will require consistent effort and conscious techniques, but the pay-off, an unshakeable bond between your kids, makes it worth it.

Preparing for a New Addition to the Family

The anticipation of adding a new member to the family can be filled with a mix of emotions ranging from sheer excitement to anxiety. It's a thrilling journey embarking on the path of expanding your family, but it's crucial to handle it with love, patience, and strategic planning, particularly when there are older children involved.

Successful sibling relationships begin before the baby even arrives. The groundwork you lay during this preparation period sets the foundation for lifelong bonds. The key to a smooth transition is creating an atmosphere of inclusion and reassurance, ensuring your older child or children that a new addition brings more love, not less.

Begin by having age-appropriate conversations with your child about the new sibling. Keep these dialogues positive and catchy. Explain the joys of having a little brother or sister and the privilege of being an older sibling. Validate any concerns and assure them you'll be there to support them through this transition.

Reading can also be a powerful tool in preparing your child for a new sibling. Consider getting children's books that tell stories about welcoming a new baby into the family. These books can help your child visualize scenarios, understand feelings better, and even identify themselves in the story.

Involve your older child in the preparation process. This involvement may include setting up the baby's room, picking out a few baby clothes, or choosing a favorite toy to give to the new baby. Not only does this foster excitement, but it also gives your child a sense of ownership and participation.

Remember to focus on your child's new role as a sibling rather than on the departing status as an only child. Talk to them about what they may teach the baby, reinforce the importance of their role, and build anticipation about their new big sibling status.

Another important consideration is timing when it comes to delivering the news. Every child is different, so it's important to consider their personality and daily routine. It might not be the best idea to introduce this big idea in the middle of other changes in their life. Stability will provide them with the security they need to accept this new update positively.

Recognize that there may be an array of reactions when you first break the news to your children about the new addition. These could range from excitement to worry, indifference to curiosity, or even anger. Regardless of their initial reaction, it's crucial to keep open lines of communication. Encourage them to express their feelings and respond with patience and understanding.

As the due date approaches, also prepare your child for your absence when you go to the hospital. Make sure to reassure them that they'll be loved and cared for even when you're not around. Prioritize setting expectations and establishing routines, so they know what to expect.

One important aspect is nurturing your relationship with your older child while waiting for the new family member. Have a special day out, create opportunities for one-on-one time, and create memories. This is not to say goodbye to your time together, but to assure them that they are still loved and cherished.

Remember, patience is key. It's okay for kids to take some time to adjust to the idea of a new sibling. What seems like regression or acting out can be quite normal and can be helped with love, patience, and reassurance. Let them process the news at their own pace.

Finally, celebrating the arrival of the new sibling will help your older child feel excited and wonderful about the baby. Throw a small "big brother" or "big sister" party. Not only will this lift your child's spirits, but also empower them for their new role. At the end of the day, your attention and assurance are what will make this transition smooth, successful, and respectful of everyone's feelings.

Preparation is paramount to ensure your firstborn transitions smoothly into the role of an older sibling. It might seem like a tricky path to navigate, but rest assured, your empathy, patience, and love will guide you in fostering the first steps towards a strong sibling bond.

The Crucial First Interactions

The first chapter of siblinghood dramatically sets the tone for the story to unfold, and nothing is more pivotal in this chapter than the very first interactions. It's not just another marker in your family's timeline; it's the inception of a relationship that will be foundational throughout your kids' lives.

So, what can you do to make these early moments as positive and meaningful as possible? Let's explore those crucial first interactions and how they can create a strong foundation for a beautiful sibling bond.

The stage for the first meeting of your children needs careful, considerate preparation. This isn't simply introducing new roommates, but instead introducing lifelong companions. It might seem cute to make the older child feel like they're meeting their new playmate. However, it's important to ensure they understand that the baby will need lots of care and attention.

Give attention to your firstborn in this process. After all, their world is about to change dramatically. The home that was once only theirs will now be shared. Include them in the preparation process for the new family member. This will help to foster feelings of importance and involvement rather than pushing them aside.

When the day arrives for the siblings to meet, try to arrange the meeting in a familiar and neutral setting. This could be a room at home, away from the new baby's crib or play area. The idea is to ensure that your first child doesn't feel invaded in their own space.

Now comes the moment when your older child gets to lay eyes on their younger sibling for the very first time. To make this moment as memorable and positive as possible, ensure that either parent (or both if possible) is holding the baby. This helps create a sense of unity and shared possession.

This first interaction should be warm, slow-paced and as tranquil as possible. Too much excitement can be overwhelming for your older child and potentially discomforting for the newborn. Just like adults, children need calm environments to process significant emotional events.

Use this time to gently explain the new dynamic – now they're an older sibling, they've got someone who will look up to them. Someone who will learn from them. This can give your older child a sense of responsibility and pride.

Understanding should be your word of the day. Try and remember, this is also a new moment for your older child. They may feel a complex mix of curiosity, excitement, or even resentment towards this stranger who has come into their home. Allow them to express these feelings freely and reassure them that it's perfectly okay to feel this way.

In the days that follow, involve your older child in caring for the baby. They can help fetch diapers, assist during bath time, or simply talk and sing to the baby. Nothing nurtures bonds better than shared experiences and shared responsibilities.

Praise your older child when they interact positively with the baby. This will leave them with positive emotional associations, encouraging them to engage more with the baby. However, take care to balance your praises with affectionate actions. The last thing you want to happen is your older child to equate being loved with taking care of their little sibling.

Finally, remember to maintain some alone time with your older child. After the introduction of a new sibling, they might suddenly feel invisible as attention shifts towards the baby. So, ensure they know that they're just as loved and cherished as before.

In the grand tapestry of family dynamics, these first interactions might seem ephemeral. But, they are the unspoken prologue, the silent start that sets the course for the journey ahead. These initial encounters, handled with care, compassion, and understanding, can breathe life into a beautiful sibling connection that withstands time and tides.

Fostering Early Bonds: Tips and Techniques

As we explored in the previous section, those initial interactions between siblings set up the groundwork for a lifelong relationship. That said, it's crucial to foster healthy sibling bonds, even in the earliest stages of that relationship. Here are some valuable tips and techniques to aid you on this rewarding journey.

First, consider introducing your elder child to the concept of siblings early on. Read picture books about families that are about to welcome a new baby. This can help your eldest child understand what to expect and begin to familiarize them with the idea of having a brother or sister before the new addition arrives.

Second, involve your older child in preparations for the baby. Take them with you when you shop for baby items and let them feel invested in the process by picking out something special for the new sibling. Carve out time for them to help set up the nursery. Sharing these moments creates a feeling of ownership and active partaking in the change happening within the family.

Third, make sure your eldest child knows that they're still important and loved. When the baby arrives, it's easy for the elder siblings to feel left out or less loved. Balance your attention between the baby and your eldest. Time spent alone with them, showing them that they're still important to you, can significantly impact how they see their new sibling.

It's not uncommon for older siblings to have mixed emotions about a new baby, and these feelings can sometimes lead to regressive behavior like tantrums or baby talk. They may suddenly act this way because they see the attention the baby's getting and are trying to compete for it.

The fourth crucial tip is to acknowledge their emotions. Let your older child know it's okay to feel upset or jealous. Recognize their feelings, and reassure them that it's natural to have mixed emotions about a new sibling. Emphasize that it's a big adjustment for everyone in the family.

Fifth, encourage the older sibling to play an active role. Even small responsibilities, like bringing a diaper or a new set of clothes for the baby, can help the older sibling feel involved and valued. This role not only fosters responsibility but also allows them to develop a sense of care and affection for their younger sibling.

Another strategy is to foster traditions and rituals that involve all your children. This could be a weekly family game night or a daily bedtime story where everyone cuddles up together. This practice nurtures a sense of belonging and creates shared memories that bind your children together.

Your direct modeling plays a significant role as well. How you interact with others, how you manage your emotions, and how you solve disputes, all play a crucial part in shaping how your children treat each other and others outside the family. Being a conscious model for your children holds a tremendous impact, so aiming to show compassion, understanding, and respectful dialogue, will help your children develop those habits as well.

Finally, adopt a patient and understanding approach when sibling disputes occur. These disagreements are a part of learning how to interact effectively with others. Shaping the way these disagreements are handled can teach invaluable lessons about empathy, compromise, negotiation skills, and conflict resolution.

Remember, fostering a bond between siblings is a dynamic and ongoing process. There will be moments filled with laughter and shared joy, as well as episodes of jealousy and disputes. That's just how sibling relationships function. Though it might be full of ups and downs, the resulting bond will serve as a valuable support and friendship that lasts their entire life.

Step by step, these practices can help your children develop a healthy sibling relationship anchored on mutual respect, understanding, and affection. Each child and each relationship is unique, so adapt these strategies to meet your family's needs. The most crucial aspect is to remain consistent, encouraging, and open-minded as you guide and nurture the sibling bond from its early stages onwards.

With intention, kindness, and a little patience, you'll foster a sibling bond designed to withstand the test of time. A bond filled with shared memories, mutual respect, and an ingrained sense of camaraderie that will stand tall amidst life's inevitable storms. So, kick start this journey of fostering bonds, and witness the magical unfolding of a lifelong friendship.

Chapter 3: Understanding Sibling Rivalries

Now that we've taken a historical perspective on siblinghood and laid the groundwork for fostering early bonds, let's delve into the heart of one of the most challenging parental hurdles – sibling rivalries. At its core, sibling rivalry stems from the natural competition solicited by limited resources – parental attention, space, toys, and, as they grow older, even social privileges. However, the areas of comparison extend to personalities, achievements, and developmental milestones that fuel these rivalries, stirring emotions and behaviors ranging from innocent mischief to rampant resentment. Sibling conflicts are not merely petty squabbles that will resolve themselves over time; they're unique opportunities for parents to teach lessons on fairness, empathy, and respect. Missing out on these lessons lead to strained relationships. Dealing with these rivalries involves identifying common triggers such as rivalry over perceived disparity in treatment or issues related to sharing, and addressing them with active listening, open conversations, and simple strategies, such as setting rules and boundaries or encouraging turn-taking. This chapter also targets age gaps and developmental differences that add another layer of complexity to sibling dynamics. Remember, every child grows at their own pace and will exhibit unique strengths, weaknesses, and preferences. It's essential to remind your children that these differences don't translate to lesser or greater love; they merely reflect the distinct place each child holds in the family mosaic. Navigating through sibling rivalries is less about extinguishing the fire of competition - a nearly impossible task — but more of guiding it into a more constructive, compassionate understanding of how to relate to another person — a skill that will arm them powerfully, not just for their sibling interactions, but for relationships they'll cultivate throughout life.

Origins of Competition and Comparison

As we delve into the foundations of sibling rivalry, it's paramount for us to understand origins of competition and comparison in the family setting. The birth order forms the basis of competition and comparison, with siblings often vying for parental attention and affirmation.

Our first point of discussion is the birth order theory, proposed by eminent psychologist Alfred Adler. According to this theory, the order in which children are born significantly impacts their personality and behavior. Firstborns tend to be responsible and eager to please, while younger siblings may exhibit a more rebellious streak as they strive to differentiate themselves from their older counterparts.

The birth order acts as a natural catalyst for competition and comparison as the fight for resources begins. In this context, resources refer to parental time, attention, and capacities. Every child instinctively desires to be favored and cherished, and as such, rivalry builds up when they feel their 'share' of parental resources is threatened by the presence of siblings.

Let's reflect upon a typical family dynamic: a second child is often compared to the elder sibling- their academic performance, athleticism, artistic abilities, and even their eating habits could come under scrutiny. And what follows, quite naturally, is a sense of competition - the younger one feels the urge to outperform their sibling to maintain their own unique identity.

This being said, comparing children's abilities and accomplishments may seem like an easy pitfall for many. It might feel natural to use an older child as a benchmark for the younger one to strive towards. However, comparison can fuel feelings of inadequacy and resentment. Each child is unique in their right and they should learn to celebrate these individual differences rather than view them as competition.

It's interesting how these competitions and comparisons are not confined to abilities and achievements but also extend to physical appearance, personal inclinations, and even choice of friends. At times, these contests radicalize sibling bonds; at other times, they act as bonding exercises during a shared journey of self-discovery.

A key trigger behind these fluctuations is the developmental stage at which the siblings are, which we will delve into later. Teenage years, specifically, bring along a whole new set of challenges including body image issues, peer pressure, and burgeoning romantic interests. Such emotionally charged phases heighten the sense of competition and comparison between siblings.

On the flip side, in many cultures, the norm is to perceive the eldest sibling not as competition, but as a secondary caregiver or a role model. That doesn't mean competition and comparison are totally eliminated. Instead, it morphs into a different form, more educative perhaps than combative. Here, the competition to be the 'best' often involves the eldest leading by example, and the younger ones striving to match up.

Siblings of the same gender can also face heightened competition, as they are more likely to be compared by others and themselves in almost every aspect - looks, abilities, and even the milestones they achieve in life. This can create a pressure-cooker environment where achievements are constantly held against one another, intensifying feelings of rivalry.

Favoritism, whether perceived or real, contributes significantly to sibling competition too. Children are quick to notice if one of them is being favored over others, leading to feelings of injustice and sparking off competition.

While competition and comparison are innate aspects of human behavior, as parents, your objective is to make sure these feelings don't lead to resentment. It's important to affirm to your kids that they are loved for who they are, not in comparison to their sibling.

Therefore, acknowledging the root causes of sibling competition and comparison is the first step in managing it effectively. Armed with this understanding, parents can mitigate feelings of rivalry, by encouraging each child's unique strengths and celebrating their individuality.

Above all, instilling a sense of security in your children can mitigate the emergence of competitive feelings. Providing ample love, care, and attention to each child ensures they don't resort to competing for these essentials. Normalize the idea of having different strengths and weaknesses. Ensure your children know that they don't need to compete with each other for your approval or love.

Remember, fostering a healthy sibling relationship is a journey- one that requires understanding and gentle guidance. Your role is more of a facilitator, helping your children turn sibling competition into camaraderie. Indeed, the resulting sibling bond can be among the most treasured relationships of their lives.

Common Triggers and How to Address Them

Encouraging a harmonic relationship between siblings becomes simpler when you can anticipate the common triggers of sibling rivalries and disputes. Identifying these triggers will not only help you understand your child's feelings better but also provide you with strategies to address and prevent conflicts. Let's dig into the common grounds of sibling disagreements and explore how they can be addressed.

Sharing: Sharing often proves to be a significant trigger for disputes among young children. The concept of sharing, whether it's toys, attention, or time, can be challenging for young minds to understand. To tackle this common trigger, instill the values of sharing and generosity early on. Use real-life situations to demonstrate the importance and benefits of sharing. This approach will help your children grasp the concept and practice sharing willingly.

Jealousy and Competition: It's natural for siblings to compare themselves to each other, fueling feelings of jealousy and competition. This can be managed by teaching your children to appreciate their own strengths and value diversity in skill sets. Additionally, making an effort to spend quality one-on-one time with each child can help them feel individually noticed and appreciated, reducing jealousy.

Space Intrusion: Especially as children grow older, intrusions into personal space can incite squabbles. Teaching your children to respect each other's space and privacy helps address this issue. Clear boundaries regarding their own personal space and belongings encourage understanding and mutual respect.

Differing Interests: In households with a wide range of ages, differing interests and developmental levels can trigger conflict. Emphasize the importance of respecting others' interests and hobbies, even if they differ. This can lead to mutual respect and even shared experiences they wouldn't have had otherwise.

Seeking Parental Attention: It's common for siblings to vie for their parents' attention, which, if not addressed, might lead to destructive behavior. Ensure that you distribute your time, attention, and affection evenly among all your children. Show them that every child in the family is equally loved and valued.

Tattling and Betrayal: Children may struggle with understanding when it's necessary to inform parents about a sibling's behavior. Drawing a clear line between seeking help and unnecessary tattling can minimize feelings of betrayal. This empowers children to problem-solve disputes independently, with the confidence that parents are there for crucial issues.

Change in Family Dynamics: Any shakeup in the family dynamic, such as a new baby, divorce, or a move can trigger tensions among siblings. Ensuring open communication during these times of transition can help. Encourage your children to express how they feel about the changes and reassure them through consistent routines and reassurances of your love.

Privileges and Responsibilities: Issues can arise around perceptions of differing privileges and responsibilities. Being transparent about why certain decisions are made can help children understand and accept these necessary differences.

These are just a few of the primary triggers for sibling rivalry and conflict. Every family and every child is unique, presenting their range of triggers. However, the key to addressing all these issues lies in open communication, measured responses, fairness, respect for individuality, and demonstrating unwavering affection.

Navigating through these triggers can indeed be challenging, but the roadmap to better sibling relationships lies in these challenges. While conflicts are an inevitable part of sibling dynamics, handling them effectively contributes enormously to the development of their mutual respect and love.

Addressing these common triggers is not about achieving a conflict-free relationship amongst siblings. Rather, it's about equipping your children with the tools they need to handle disputes healthfully and maturely. The goal is to cultivate a familial environment where disagreements do not deteriorate into resentment.

As we move forward, we will delve deeper into strategies and practices for establishing harmony in the home. Learning to set fair boundaries, establish rules, and cultivate mutual respect and understanding is a beautiful journey to embark on, resulting in a stronger bond between your children.

Our next section will focus on Navigating Age Gaps and Developmental Differences, where we delve into managing relationships between siblings of different ages and stages. Remember, each step taken with love, intention, and consistency brings you closer to fostering a serene home environment and nurturing lifelong friendships between your children.

Navigating Age Gaps and Developmental Differences

As you dive deeper into the world of sibling relationships, it's important to acknowledge one crucial factor that influences these dynamics: age gaps and developmental differences. These differences aren't merely about the number of years apart but also the stages of cognitive and emotional development siblings might be in.

When children are close in age, there's potential for both companionship and competition. They might share similar interests, fostering common ground, but these similarities can lead to rivalry. Alternatively, wider age gaps can produce a protective older sibling dynamic but might also cultivate feelings of detachment due to differing interests.

Understanding these challenges isn't about labeling one age gap as 'ideal' and another as 'problematic.' It's not a judgment on your family planning. Rather, it's about aiding you with the necessary insights to nurture healthy relationships across varying sibling dynamics.

Firstly, let's begin with the foundation of empathy. If your older child mocks or becomes frustrated with their younger sibling's inability to share or understand certain rules, use it as an opportunity for an empathetic conversation. Explain to them that their sibling is still learning and that there were times when they, too, didn't know how to share or follow rules. Reminding them of their early years fosters empathy and patience towards the younger ones.

Next, discuss the concept of fairness. Often children assess fairness in terms of sameness. If siblings have different bedtimes, for example, the younger might protest this as 'not fair' because it's not the same. Parents need to help children understand that fairness means everyone getting what they need, which might look different for each family member. This perspective can ease feelings of unfair treatment tied to developmental differences.

Furthermore, finding common activities for siblings with substantial age gaps can be challenging. It's quite possible that the 8-year-old is not excited about tea parties as the 3-year-old is. In those cases, try to find a middle ground — activities that all ages enjoy. Family game nights, nature walks, or simply reading together can lay down a framework of shared experiences and memories.

If vast differences in interests persist, consider 'shared-care' activities. Perhaps your eldest can read to the younger ones or assist them with a craft project. This not only keeps the kids engaged together but also fosters a sense of responsibility amongst the older ones.

Birth order also plays into these dynamics, and roles can inadvertently get reinforced over the years: the responsible eldest, the attention-seeking middle child, the pampered youngest. It might seem innocuous, but these stereotypes can limit the individuality of your children. Occasionally mix things up. Let the youngest lead an activity or ask the eldest for help. Encourage children to see themselves, not just as older or younger, but as individuals with unique abilities.

It's also important for parents to avoid comparing their children's skills and accomplishments. Remarks like "Your older brother was reading at your age" can be harmful, producing resentment between siblings and undermining their confidence. Every child develops at their own pace, and it's essential to respect and encourage their individual journey.

Teenagers and toddlers under one roof may present unique challenges, but also opportunities for incredible sibling bonds. High schoolers can help care for little ones, forming a unique bond in the process. The balance here is to ensure the older child doesn't feel burdened with excessive responsibility, and the younger one doesn't feel dominated.

In blended families, kids may come with existing sibling relationships that can undergo massive shifts. There may be anger, resentment, or feelings of being ignored when a new sibling arrives. Acknowledging these feelings and navigating them with patience and open dialogue can aid in the transition.

In the case of twins or multiples, there's a unique dynamic at play where siblings are also peers developmentally. They grow and learn together, creating a deep bond but also intense rivalry. Encourage their individuality while acknowledging their exceptional connection.

Remember, there isn't a one-size-fits-all answer when it comes to sibling dynamics. There'll be bouts of bickering and instances of heartwarming affection. As parents, your role is to guide and nurture these relationships while steering them towards mutual respect, empathy, and appreciation of their shared history and individual uniqueness.

Invariably, as with any family, age gaps and developmental differences will offer both challenges and opportunities. It's about helping your children navigate these realities and cultivate stronger bonds. The journey might be bumpy, but the destination of a supportive, loving sibling relationship is worth all the ups and downs.

Chapter 4: Strategies for Harmony in the Home

As we move from understanding sibling rivalries, it's time for us to delve into the crux of creating a harmonious environment within the home. This chapter will shed light on implementing rules, boundaries and standards of fair play that foster a sense of justice and equality among the youngsters. It's essential that these standards aren't just words on a wall, but rather living, breathing elements of the daily routine within the household. Cultivate an environment of mutual respect and understanding by acknowledging each child's feelings and thoughts, helping siblings see each other's perspectives and reminding them that respect is a two-way street. In addition, engage your children in collaborative activities and shared goals. Activities for leisure or everyday responsibilities, when done together, can teach children about teamwork, compromise, and the pleasure of shared victory. It's important not to enforce harmony; instead, provide the guidelines and let your children navigate their way to harmony using these valuable tools.

Rules, Boundaries, and Fair Play

Developing harmony within a home is like choreographing a captivating performance - it requires thoughtfulness, precision, and a lot of practice. It's essential to establish rules and boundaries, which guide the interactions between siblings, while maintaining fair play among them. This can serve as a beacon, illuminating the path towards relationships built on respect and understanding.

From the outset, it's important to set clear and consistent rules that apply to everyone. Vague or inconsistent rules can cause confusion and disagreements. Whether it's about sharing toys, screen time limits, bedtime routines, or household chores, it's critical that every child understands what is expected of them. However, remember that rules should not be overly rigid or stifling; they should aim to foster a peaceful, respectful and harmonious environment.

Boundaries, in the context of sibling relationships, are equally important. They bring a level of respect and understanding to the relationship that is crucial for its development. Each child needs and deserves their own space, mentally, physically, and emotionally. It needs to be clear to all siblings that invading these spaces without consent is not acceptable.

With boundaries in place, consider utilizing personal belongings and personal spaces as the first steps towards understanding. Each child should have their own possessions and a place in the house they can call their own, even if it's as simple as their own drawer or shelf. This can instill respect for personal boundaries and ownership from an early age.

It's important to remember that treating children fairly does not equate to treating them exactly the same. Each child, their needs, their traits, and their circumstances, should be acknowledged as unique. Fairness is not about silencing these differences under a blanket of uniformity, but about recognizing and accommodating this diversity.

Praise and punishment, two points of contention in many sibling relationships, should also be meted out fairly. Consistent criteria for administering rewards and consequences allow children to understand what is expected and appreciate that rules aren't arbitrary.

In the quest for fair play, parents can champion the importance of sportsmanship. Just like in sports, where respect for fellow players and umpires is part of the game, children can be taught to play fair in the game of life, and this includes interactions with siblings. Encourage them to display empathy, respect for each other, and to celebrate their victories together.

Conflict resolution strategies play a vital part in maintaining fair play. Disputes are inevitable, and it's crucial that children know how to resolve them constructively. Rather than stepping in to solve every disagreement, allow siblings to mediate their own problems to an extent. This fosters negotiation and understanding, both invaluable life skills.

Being a good role model as a parent is important. Children often take cues from their parents, imitating their way of handling conflicts, their respect for others, and their honor of boundaries. When they see you treating everyone fairly and respecting individual boundaries, they are more likely to emulate these behaviors.

Remember, the aim is not to create a cold environment of strict regulation, but to cultivate a home where siblings feel secure and respected. Regular family meetings can provide a platform where everyone can air their views, discuss changes to rules, express their feelings, and participate in making decisions. This not only reinforces the rules and boundaries, but also promotes open, honest communication.

Help kids understand that as they grow older, rules and boundaries may change. As your children mature and their circumstances change, adjustments may be necessary. This also gives them something to look forward to, recognizing that greater age brings more freedom and responsibility.

Raising multiple children can indeed be a balancing act, but establishing clear rules, setting firm boundaries, and promoting fairness can help create a supportive atmosphere. Further, these values will stay with your children, guiding them in their relationships outside the home.

While it requires effort, time, and patience, setting these ground rules can make the journey smoother. And when everyone abides by these, it promotes an atmosphere of mutual respect where love and understanding can flourish.

In conclusion, rules, boundaries, and fair play serve as three pillars on which strong sibling bonds can be built. They provide the structure necessary for these relationships to thrive in a nurturing and respectful environment. And, these aren't just about managing the present but also providing the necessary tools your children will need to navigate their relationships in the world outside.

Cultivating Mutual Respect and Understanding

The foundation of any harmonious sibling relationship lies in mutual respect and understanding. The elements of respect and acknowledgment of each child's unique perspective can truly create a lifelong bond. This section will delve into the practices and strategies that can help parents foster such respect and understanding within their family.

Navigating through the dynamics of sibling relationships requires empathy and finesse from parents. It's crucial to remember that every child is a universe in themselves, carrying their unique blend of strengths, passions, fears, and dreams. When siblings learn to respect these differences and understand each other's perspectives, their bond strengthens.

Now, the first concept to delve into is the idea of 'mutual respect.' What this means is acknowledgments of each child's feelings, thoughts, needs, and space. To cultivate this atmosphere, it is essential for parents to set the tone themselves. Your behavior, expressions of feelings, and response to their emotions form the first manual of social dynamics for your children. When you demonstrate respect towards their feelings, they learn to extend the same to others.

Mutual respect doesn't merely mean politeness or basic courtesy; it goes beyond that. It's about teaching your children that every individual is unique and has their own set of ideas and opinions, which should be respected even if they differ from their own. It's about guiding them towards understanding this diversity leads to richer interactions and opportunities to learn from each other.

It is important to instill in your children that just as they are unique and special, so are their siblings. They need to understand that their sibling's thoughts and feelings matter just as much as their own. They must learn to empathize with their sibling's feelings and develop a sense of 'perspective understanding.' It's about the ability to view situations from their sibling's viewpoint to genuinely understand their reactions and emotions.

This 'perspective understanding' can indeed seem complex, especially to younger children. Therefore, parents need to guide children gently towards this concept. You could use situations around you, stories, or even role-playing to help them get a grasp of different perspectives. Remember, the objective is to help them understand the diversity of thoughts, and there's no 'right' or 'wrong' perspective, just differences.

Next comes the acknowledgment of personal space. Children need to understand the importance of respecting each other's physical and emotional space. Just like adults, children too have boundaries that must be respected. Physical boundaries could be about respecting personal belongings, while emotional boundaries could mean understanding when a sibling needs some alone time or has an emotional difficulty they would rather not discuss. By teaching your children to respect each other's space and boundaries, you are helping them create a healthy relationship dynamic that carries forward into adulthood.

Now, let's discuss misunderstandings. They are inevitable in any relationship. However, it's essential to handle them in a manner that promotes respect and understanding. Acknowledge all sides of the conflict without bias, and encourage open and honest communication. Allow your children to express their feelings, ask questions, and bring suggestions for resolving the conflict.

Another essential factor is inclusivity and fairness. It is vital to ensure every child feels included, cherished, and equally important. Avoid showing favoritism as it breeds resentment. Treat each child's achievements, challenges, and emotions with equal importance. Regular family activities and discussions where each child gets an equal say can do wonders.

Finally, parent's attitudes and reactions play a key role in cultivating mutual respect and understanding among siblings. Your way of interacting with your kids, resolving conflicts, handling emotions truly sets the stage. Make it a habit to listen carefully, respond respectfully to your child's concerns. Show compassion when they make mistakes and give them room to learn and grow.

Teaching your children mutual respect and understanding is a patience-testing task, but the results are undoubtedly rewarding. As they learn to communicate effectively, empathize with each other, respect differences, and peacefully resolve conflicts, you'll certainly find tranquility and harmony in your family relationships.

In this journey, remember that it's crucial to provide love, guidance, and a listening ear but also give them space to figure things out. This delicate balance is the secret to fostering strong, affectionate, and lifelong sibling relationships.

As we delve deeper into the strategies for harmony in the home, the next section will guide you towards introducing collaborative activities and shared goals that could strengthen mutual respect and understanding among siblings further.

Introducing Collaborative Activities and Shared Goals

The foundation for a harmonious home has been laid; now it's time to build. The next chapter of our journey takes us to the world of collaborative activities and shared goals. Structuring time together in a purposeful and goal-oriented way can work wonders in strengthening your children's bonds with each other. Just as bricks need mortar to stick together, your children need these shared experiences to form the glue of their relationship.

When interactive activities become a part of your family's routine, they create opportunities for siblings to understand each other's strengths, weaknesses, likes, and dislikes. These activities are the perfect ecosystem where mutual respect blooms and flourishes among your children.

But what exactly are collaborative activities? They are activities designed to require collective efforts. They need involvement and participation from all siblings to successfully complete them. An excellent example is when you ask your children to put away their toys together after playtime or work on an art project jointly.

The most crucial aspect to remember is that the activity should be engaging enough that all participating siblings enjoy it. Use these as opportunities for your children to learn to negotiate, compromise, and divide tasks based on their individual strengths.

Shared goals, on the other hand, are objectives set for your children to achieve collectively. Here's where planning family trips, starting a garden, or even setting up a lemonade stand comes in. These aren't instantaneous tasks but provide an ongoing, collective sense of purpose, fostering an environment of teamwork and strengthening sibling ties.

Now, that's not to say that collaborative activities and shared goals don't have their share of hurdles. However, you, as a parent, can cleverly navigate these hurdles. For instance, what happens when one child loses interest or another one wants to dominate the activity? Simple, modify the activity to cater to individual likes or evenly divide the responsibilities to ensure fair participation.

One of the hallmarks of successful collaborative activities is their exclusivity to foster shared experiences. Bake a cake together, build a fort, or collaborate on a craft project; the underlying spirit is to achieve something together, whether tangible like a batch of cookies or intangible like the sense of accomplishment.

Remember that these activities are not a covert discipline or instruction session. Aim for them to be enjoyable. Use them as an opportunity to show your kids that everyone's contribution is valuable, no matter how different. Success will look different every time. It's not always about getting the perfect end product; it's about the process and bonding that goes along with it.

It's also critical to introduce shared goals gradually. Launching too many shared goals all at once can overwhelm your children. Take it slow; start off with a simple shared goal like working together to keep their playroom clean or taking turns caring for the family pet. With time, move on to more complex projects.

Allowing your children to play a part in setting these goals also empowers them. This makes them feel more invested in the outcome and encourages them to work harder at achieving the goal. Moreover, involving them in the process of decision-making promotes respect for each other's choices and perspectives.

Don't worry about whether the collaborative activities usefully occupy every minute of your child's free time or if every shared goal is a major milestone. The primary aim is to foster heartwarming, shared experiences which mold their underlying relationship and sculpt the foundations of their lifelong bonds.

Remember to keep it fun, keep it fair, and maintain a balance. Encourage teamwork, but don't impose it. The goal is not just cooperation and collaboration, but also establishing connections that stay strong and fruitful throughout their lives.

You can introduce a multitude of activities and goals without stifling their individual interests. Let your children see that even within unity, they can retain, celebrate, and honor their uniqueness. Using collaborative activities and shared goals, your home can be a thriving hub of bustling, lively interactions, slowly but surely building a harmonious symphony of sibling love and respect.

With every giggling whisper during their shared activities and every proud smile when they accomplish a shared goal, your children are learning the essence of togetherness and the joy of companionship – lessons they'll cherish for a lifetime.

Chapter 5:
Communication is Key

Building on the strategies for creating harmony in our homes we've discussed in the previous section, we're now entering an essential part of the sibling relationship: communication. It's known that words carry weight. What your children say to each other can leave a mark—whether that mark is positive or negative depends largely on how communication is modeled and encouraged within your family. There's a need to foster active listening skills not just in parents, but also in siblings. This skill enables them to truly understand the perspectives of their siblings, rather than simply hearing what was said. Addressing concerns and handling disputes is another crucial aspect of sibling communication. It's important to create a safe space where each child feels heard and understood, and where conflicts can be resolved effectively. Lastly, remember to encourage positive talk - through praise and affectionate words - between your children. Kids often learn how to talk to their siblings from how their parents communicate with them and with each other. So, take this chapter as a reminder to lead by example; your own communication habits may shape the way your kids interact with each other.

Active Listening Skills for Parents and Siblings

Active listening is a powerful tool for fostering understanding and empathy within a family. It might sound simple, but in reality, it's more than just letting another person speak without interruption. It's about truly understanding, validating and responding to the speaker's feelings and thoughts.

Parents often feel that they need to swoop in with advice when their children express fears, frustrations, or disappointments. While offering guidance is important, sometimes, what children need more is for their feelings to be recognized and validated. Active listening plays a crucial role in this process.

Let's consider how this plays out in a practical example. Your two children are arguing over a toy. Instead of catering to the one who is crying the loudest, you might practice active listening by saying, "I can see that you both really want this toy. Let's take turns saying why it's important to us."

By doing this, you're giving both children an equal platform to express their feelings, validating their emotions, and teaching a crucial lesson on respect and understanding.

Moreover, active listening isn't just limited to disputes or conflict. It's an excellent skill to utilize during everyday conversations and casual chats. Doing so helps children feel heard and promotes open, honest communication.

Next, it's important to remember that active listening isn't complete without responding adequately. Reflect back what's been said by summarizing or paraphrasing, and ask clarifying questions if needed. By doing so, you confirm your understanding and show respect to the speaker.

Don't forget the non-verbal cues. Our body language often conveys more than words ever can. Keep eye contact, lean forward, and offer nodding gestures as signs of understanding. These cues show the speaker that you're fully present and invested in the conversation.

How can siblings engage in active listening? Just as we advise parents to be attentive listeners, we should encourage siblings to do the same. Encourage your children to listen to each other, show empathy, and respond appropriately. This fosters a nurturing environment for your children, enhancing mutual respect and cooperation among siblings.

Remember, modeling behavior is the most effective form of teaching. Let your children see you practicing active listening with them and other adults. Show them how to patiently wait their turn in conversations, empathetically respond, and respect differing viewpoints.

As children witness these positive interactions, they start adopting the same practices in their own communication. In time, this strengthens not only their sibling relationships but also their relationships outside the family.

A familiar trap parents often fall into is trying to rush or fix everything. When your child expresses distress or frustration, don't be too quick to offer solutions. Let your child process their feelings. This helps them grow emotionally and mentally. It's often more helpful to say, "I see how upset you are...let's try and work this out together."

Empathy forms the foundation of active listening. Without it, our ability to understand and connect with others is compromised. Teach your children empathy by discussing several possible feelings or perspectives brought up by conflicts or situations. This cultivates emotional intelligence and compassionate attitudes in your children.

Finally, remember to be patient. Developing active listening skills takes time for both parents and children. There'll be instances where you falter, which is perfectly okay. Improvement comes with practice and dedication. As you consistently practice active listening, you'll find communication within your family becoming more understanding, harmonious, and respectful.

In conclusion, active listening is a testament to this truth - sometimes, we don't need grand gestures or lavish gifts to show our love. Often times, it's simply about being there, offering a listening ear, and showing genuine understanding. As parents and siblings, actively listening to one another becomes the first step in laying the foundation of a strong and enduring family relationship.

Addressing Concerns and Handling Disputes

Now that we've explored the importance of effective communication, it's crucial to address an integral part of sibling relationships — conflict resolution. Even with the best of intentions and highest levels of understanding, disputes are inevitable. They aren't necessarily a bad thing; they can serve as a catalyst for growth and learning. The focus should be on effectively addressing these concerns and handling the disputes fairly and helpfully.

When concern arises within a sibling relationship, it's crucial to address it head-on. Ignoring the issue or pushing it under the rug doesn't solve the problem; in fact, it can exacerbate it. Addressing the concern means validating the feelings of all parties involved and encouraging open, honest dialogue. Stay away from taking sides, as this can foster resentment. Instead, work to understand the perspective of each child and guide them towards understanding each other.

Disputes can sometimes spin out of control, especially when tempers are high. It's essential to cool down before engaging in any conflict resolution. Encourage your children to take a break, breathe, and calm down before they discuss the issue.

This prevents the escalation of the situation and promotes a more productive dialogue.

The art of compromise is another integral part of dispute resolution. Sometimes, it's not about who's right or wrong, but finding a middle ground everyone can agree on. Encourage your children to consider their sibling's needs and come up with solutions that are acceptable to all parties involved.

During these discussions, it's essential to maintain a safe environment where everyone feels their opinions are valued and respected. If one child feels threatened or judged, they may retreat or become defensive. This vilification can derail the purpose of open conversation and solution-seeking.

Active listening skills, which we talked about earlier in this book, can be a game-changer in handling disputes. Teaching your children to fully listen and understand their sibling's perspective can lead to empathy and a willingness to work towards a solution.

It's also necessary to foster an environment where mistakes are viewed as learning opportunities. If a child's mistake leads to a dispute, use the incident as an opportunity to teach problem-solving skills. Instead of focusing on the fault, concentrate on how to correct the problem and prevent it from reoccurring in the future.

As the parent in the situation, remember to model excellent conflict resolution skills. Reflect on how you handle and resolve conflicts in your own life. Your kids are always watching and learning from you, so it's essential to depict the strategies you want them to adopt.

In cases where disputes become heated or don't seem to have a solution, it might help to bring in a neutral third party. This person could be a trusted family friend, member of the extended family, or a professional counselor. The third party can help mediate, provide perspective, and guide your children toward resolution.

Predetermine consequences of conflicts that escalate to harmful levels. If a dispute becomes physical, or in extreme cases, abusive, having predetermined consequences can help limit these instances. The severity of the consequences should parallel the seriousness of the conflict. Having these rules in place will act as a deterrent while teaching your kids about the unpleasant outcomes of harmful conflicts.

Beyond just resolving the disputes, it's also essential to reflect on them. Reflecting allows everyone involved to learn from the experience, understand the triggers, and find ways to avoid similar disputes in the future.

Lastly, don't forget that everybody, including parents, is learning. Sometimes mistakes will be made—the key to remember is not to be hard on yourself or your kids. Be resilient, pick up where you went wrong, and try again, with the goal of harmonious sibling relationships always in sight.

Addressing concerns and handling disputes effectively is a skill that comes with practice and patience. With intention and effort, you will equip your children with valuable tools that will serve them in their relationships throughout their lives.

Encouraging Positive Talk Between Siblings

The goal isn't just to resolve immediate disputes between siblings; it's also to cultivate life-long positive communication habits. This chapter is going to broaden your tool kit for promoting positivity and understanding in sibling conversations.

Start simple. Encourage siblings to compliment one another. It may seem trivial, but cultivating an environment where kind words often flow can greatly boost morale and improve relationships. When one of your children does something praiseworthy, suggest to another sibling to compliment them.

Make respect a compulsory element of communication within your household. Explain to your children what respect means, and model it in your interactions with both them and other adults. Reinforce the message that hearing each other out, no matter the circumstances, is a non-negotiable rule of conversation.

Words are incredible tools for building relationships, but don't underestimate the power of body language. Teach your children about the importance of non-verbal communication such as eye contact, facial expressions, and gestures. Explain how these can either enhance or contradict the words spoken.

Create a culture of encouragement within your home. Encourage your children to cheer each other on, whether it's in academics, sports, or personal projects. Encouragement can foster a strong foundation of mutual support and positive talk within the family.

It's also vital to teach your kids the value of giving feedback rather than criticism. Constructive feedback nourishes growth, self-awareness, and personal development. Create guidelines on giving helpful feedback and ensure it's followed during sibling-to-sibling talks.

Let your home be a safe haven for feelings. Allow your kids to express anger, disappointment, or distress freely, but make sure they understand the importance of doing so in a respectful and non-harmful manner. The objective is to avoid repressing emotions, but manage them healthily instead.

Highlight the importance of empathy in conversations. Teach your kids to place themselves in each other's shoes and understand viewpoints different from their own. This promotes compassion and helps ward off potential disputes.

Reiterate the role of honesty in healthy communication. Honesty, even when uncomfortable, fosters trust and respect. Guide your children on how to share their truthful thoughts kindly and tactfully.

The power of apology should also be emphasized. Teach your children the value of saying "I'm sorry" and accepting an apology graciously. This encourages accountability and forgiveness, which are vital elements in any relationship.

Periodically hold family meetings that nurture positive communication. Allow each child to speak their mind openly and respectfully, and make sure their points are discussed and taken into consideration. This practice will also give them a sense of being valued and heard.

Introduce the concept of thoughtful questioning to your children. When siblings ask each other questions, they show interest and reinforce bonds. Educate your kids on how to ask engaging, open-ended questions during their conversations.

Finally, you as parents play a pivotal role in the encouragement of positive talk amongst your children. Always lead by example, showcasing how you expect them to interact with one another through your interactions with family members and others.

Remember, encouraging positive talk between siblings is a continuous process and each family's journey will look different. What works for one family may not produce the same results in another. As parents, all we can do is make the consistent effort, and with time, patience, and love, we can guide our children towards fostering thoughtful and respectful communication with their siblings.

As we move on to the next chapter, we'll delve into the importance of individuality, even within family unity, and how you can foster this within your children to strengthen their bond as siblings. Let's see how important it is to celebrate each of our children's unique qualities while nurturing a tight-knit familial bond.

Chapter 6:
Fostering Individuality within Family Unity

Now that we've covered the importance of communication in building sibling bonds, it's time to look at how we can maintain the delicate balance between embracing each child's individuality and forging a strong collective family identity. Remember, your children aren't just siblings; they're unique individuals with their very own passions, talents, and dreams. It's essential to celebrate these unique qualities and achievements alongside the shared family experiences. Each child should feel seen, valued, and understood for who they truly are, not just their role within the family unit. This recognition can be as simple as praising a school accomplishment, hosting a mini celebration for a skill recently mastered, or dedicating one-on-one time with each child to hone their individual interests and talents. While it's important to have shared activities as a family, striking a balance with individual pursuits for each child can bolster their sense of self and autonomy. In fostering each child's individuality, we're not just helping them cultivate self-esteem and a confident persona; we're showing them that they can curate their life course – a lesson which would ultimately nurture a healthy appreciation of unique characteristics within their family framework and beyond.

Celebrating Unique Qualities and Achievements

In this journey through the art of fostering familial unity while still encouraging individuality, we've come across a significant premise – the celebration of unique qualities and accomplishments of each child in your brood. This chapter will walk you through the lens of recognizing, acknowledging, and celebrating the unique traits your children possess, and their individual achievements, no matter how small.

We encourage you to not just see your children as siblings but as individuals with their abilities, interests, and personalities. As parents, it is crucial to note that every child is uniquely hardwired. It's this very uniqueness that transcribes into their abilities and achievements.

Often in families, especially ones with multiple children, it's easy to compare and contrast abilities and accomplishments amongst siblings. While it's a natural instinct, steering clear from such comparisons is necessary because comparisons can often culminate in envy or animosity.

Understand that each child has a different journey, and trying to match one's journey with another's is like comparing apples with oranges. Acknowledge this difference and make a conscious effort to honor every individual journey just like how it is - unique and incomparable.

One essential aspect to recognize is that success is subjective. While society might dictate success in terms of traditional achievements like good grades or winning at sports, remember that success significantly varies at an individual level. It could be conquering the fear of dogs, making a new friend, finishing a challenging book, and so on.

As parents, if you change your perception of success, you'll notice more opportunities to celebrate your child's achievements. This celebration instills a sense of confidence and self-worth in children. It also encourages them to continue to strive and work hard in their areas of interest.

Remember, even small accomplishments matter significantly in the grand scheme of a child's growth and development. Recognizing minor achievements makes your child see that every step towards their goal is essential, and hard work does pay off, even if it's in small ways.

However, as parents, the onus is on you to strike a balance. While cherishing accomplishments is essential, it is equally important to let your children know that it's okay not to excel at everything. They should know they're loved and appreciated even when they don't necessarily "achieve" something. The crux of the matter lies in appreciating the effort your child puts in, rather than just the final outcome.

Commending effort can be a beautiful way to foster a growth mindset in children. When children realize that hard work, resilience, and perseverance are as important as the end result, they're more likely to face challenges with a positive attitude. They understand that failure is not the end but an opportunity to learn and grow.

Celebrating individual achievements also implies acknowledging the uniqueness of each child. Every child has a different strength. Let's celebrate those strengths. If one child excels in reading, let them be known for it amongst family and friends. If the other child is good at arts, cherish their creativity. This way, everyone has their own identity within the family, further reducing comparisons.

Immerse yourself in your child's interest areas, which would serve as an excellent opportunity for you to understand their world. If their passion lies in painting, sit down and paint with them. Dive deep into their realm of artistry. Showing this kind of interest develops a stronger bond between parent and child and portrays that their interests are valued in the family.

In conclusion, celebrating one's unique qualities and achievements cultivates a sense of self-worth and individuality. The celebration requires an open mind ready to appreciate any accomplishment and focus on the efforts made, not just the outcome. Your dedicated attention to their world of interests further enhances their sense of self, thus enriching their experience as an upstanding member of the family.

Remember, every child has their individual journey; they bloom at their own pace. The duty rests in our hands as parents to celebrate their blossoming, no matter when, how, or in what direction it occurs. Safe journey on this beautiful journey of parenthood, embracing individuality, and nurturing a tight-knit family unit. The celebration of each child's unique qualities and achievements truly serves as one of the cornerstones for fostering individuality within family unity.

The Importance of One-on-One Time with Each Child

Having touched on the importance of celebrating each child's unique qualities and achievements, we now delve into a crucial aspect of nurture that plays high significance in fostering individuality within the ensemble of family unity— the importance of one-on-one time with each child. As parents, constantly balancing responsibilities might make it challenging to devote individual attention to each child; however, the benefits far outweigh the challenges.

One-on-one time is more than just a window of isolation within a crowd; it's a sacred space where genuine connections are forged, understanding is deepened, and unique identities are acknowledged and validated. During these moments, parents can transform into active listeners, guides, cheerleaders, and confidants for their children.

Each child in your family has their essence, a unique blend of talents, interests, and perspectives. Spending one-on-one time with each child acknowledges these differences. You're not only saying, "I see you," but also adding, "I appreciate what makes you unique, and I love you for it."

One-on-one time with each child promotes individual self-worth. While unity within the family is undoubtedly critical, it's exceedingly essential for children to know they're valued as individuals. By dedicating some time to focus solely on one child, you convey the message that they're worth your time and attention, fostering a sense of self-esteem and reinforcing their individual importance.

The effects of this time extend to the child's emotional well-being. A study published in the Journal of Marriage and Family found a strong correlation between one-on-one time with the parent and the child's overall emotional well-being. By spending quality time with each child, you contribute to their emotional security, crucial for wholesome development.

Let's not forget how a passion for fun is ignited during these moments. One-on-one time is the perfect setting for parents and children to let loose, be silly, and engage in the pure joy of being in each other's company. By making these moments fun and enjoyable, you make lasting positive memories for both you and your child.

During these periods, children have opportunities to open up on personal feelings or concerns they might otherwise feel uncomfortable sharing. Having an open line of communication with each child is essential, and it starts with you being present, patient and empathetic.

One-on-one time also presents a chance to cultivate a child's independence. While group time often sees children following each other, one-on-one time allows them to make decisions, express their opinions, and navigate scenarios that feed their growth and maturity.

Investing one-on-one time does not mean neglecting your responsibilities or other family members. Be transparent with the other children about why you're spending individual time and ensure them that their turn is coming. this way, they'll understand it's not favoritism but fair practice.

Initiating one-on-one time can be as simple as following your child's lead, noticing their interests, and participating in their chosen activities. Whether it's a walk to the park, a game of catch, or simply reading together, the key is to be present actively and engaged.

Remember that quality matters over quantity. Your children will remember the exchange of smiles, laughter, and heartfelt moments more than they'll recall the presumed duration of time spent together.

One-on-one time fosters deeper connections, enhances mutual understanding, and strengthens bonds between parents and children. It's a delightful blending of moments where life's greatest lessons are taught and learned, where laughter is abundant, where love flourishes, and where profound memories are born. One-on-one time is, in essence, an enduring expression of love that powerfully whispers into a child's ear, "You matter."

As we continue this journey, remember to balance these individual bonding times with group activities because while the richness of individual sound is important, the melody of unity is what binds the symphony that we call family.

Balancing Group Activities and Individual Pursuits

One of the most important challenges a parent faces is balancing group activities and individual pursuits among their children. The key is learning how to thread the needle to maintain the bond that binds the family while still respecting and nurturing the children's individuality. Keep in mind that sibling relationships will unavoidably fluctuate as children grow and their interests develop and change.

Group activities have amazing benefits. They create a collaborative atmosphere where siblings learn to work together to achieve a common goal. These moments create opportunities for children to develop communication, problem-solving skills, and a sense of camaraderie. Participation in joint activities can foster memories that last a lifetime and significantly deepen the bond between siblings.

However, the value of individual pursuits cannot be understated too. Each child, just like adults, has a unique personality, strengths, and interests. You need to be cognizant that each child deserves an opportunity to embrace and cultivate these differences to thrive personally and develop a strong sense of self-worth and independence.

Understanding your children's diverse interests, strengths, and weaknesses is paramount. With that knowledge, you can guide each child in finding individual pursuits they genuinely enjoy. It could be art lessons for the kid who loves drawing, dance classes for the child with a knack for movement, or a science camp for the one with an inquisitive mind. Bear in mind that these activities should be child-led, not parent-led. We can't force our interests on our kids; they should be given the autonomy to explore and understand their individual passions.

While catering to each kid's individual pursuits is necessary, it is equally important to instill a sense of appreciation for the other sibling's interests. You can lead by example, showing interest and engaging each child in conversations about their activities. Such platform sparks curiosity among siblings about each other's activities, encourages respect, and reduces the likelihood of jealousy and rivalry.

Striking a balance between joint activities and independent pursuits is crucial, but it does not imply a 50-50 split. It would be best if you assessed the situation from time to time. For instance, during summer vacations when kids have more free time, family trips and games may be encouraged. On the other hand, the school year may offer more time for individual pursuits with extracurricular activities and assignments.

The art of creating a healthy balance essentially lies in flexibility. You need to be prepared to tweak the equilibrium based on changing circumstances, children's personal development, or even the general mood in the home. Flexibility shows your children that you are paying attention to their needs and emotions, thus making them feel loved and respected.

Remember, balancing group and individual activities isn't one-size-fits-all. Each family will have its unique rhythm and pattern. Even the child's age should be taken into consideration. Younger kids might require more communal activities while older ones might crave more independence and thus lean towards individual pursuits.

Do observe the dynamics within your family. If external activities are causing stress or internal friction, maybe it's time to cut back and focus more on the family. It's essential to ensure that the children's schedule leaves room for family connection and relaxation too. Avoid an overscheduled, stressful environment.

Moreover, individual or group activities shouldn't impede academics. Be cognizant of not jeopardizing educational responsibilities while accommodating these pursuits. Strike a fine balance between work and play to ensure that children learn the importance of commitment and time management.

The balancing act may seem daunting initially, but remember, parenting is a journey, and these challenges help us grow and evolve as caregivers. It's okay to stumble and learn along the way.

Ultimately, the aim is to provide a nurturing environment for your children to flourish both as individuals and as part of their sibling network. This balancing act, though tricky, is quite doable and can lead to the development of diverse skills, a strong sense of self, and nurturing deep bonds among siblings.

Striking this balance isn't just beneficial for your children but for the whole family. It promotes overall harmony and ensures every family member feels seen, heard, and valued. So embrace this challenge with poise and patience, and you'll have a family that respects individuality and cherishes unity.

Chapter 7:
The Teen Years and Beyond

The critical leap from childhood to adolescence brings growing independence, stronger identities, and the influences that often come with complex life situations. These dynamics often bring new challenges for siblings due to their broader perspectives, shifting priorities, and sometimes differences. As challenging as it may sound, parents can utilize these experiences to bolster the bond between their children by cultivating a deep understanding of adolescent dynamics. It's essential for parents to remain actively involved, accessible, and supportive during these stages, with discussions about future aspirations and adult responsibilities. As your children mature, their life paths may diverge due to varying interests, life choices, or simply geographical distance. Despite this, maintaining sibling connections is paramount, fostering familial ties and ensuring your children have an unwavering support system in each other. By emphasizing the importance of commitment, communication, and mutual respect, siblings can navigate the trials of life while preserving the strong bonds they formed in their earlier years.

Understanding Adolescent Dynamics

Adolescence is a period of tremendous growth and change, physically, emotionally, and everyone else involved. It can be quite challenging to understand adolescent dynamics, particularly within the sibling context, considering the uniqueness of the phase and the individual. In this section, we'll delve into the intricacies of teenage development, how they impact sibling relationships, and ways to manage and foster positive connections during this critical stage.

Typically characterized by a quest for independence and identity, teenagers often exhibit behaviors reflective of their evolving self-awareness and sense of autonomy. This is a period when they are exploring their individuality, and conflicts with siblings - who they have typically seen as components of their identity - can increasingly happen. It might seem like they're trying to break away from family bonds, but in reality, it's a significant part of their growth.

As parents, it's crucial to understand that these dynamics aren't just about rebellion. They're part of adolescents shaping their worldview. We must respect this process of self-identity while providing guidance and fostering respect for other family members. This is an important balance to strike, acknowledging their maturity, but not overlooking the important familial connections that are still forming and evolving.

In addition to their quest for independence, teenagers are experiencing significant physical, hormonal, and cognitive changes. Their brain structure is literally morphing, which can affect their behavior, perspectives, and emotions. They are likely to be more emotional, argue more, and display an all-knowing attitude. This change is normal and something to be understood, not necessarily corrected.

Another critical aspect to consider in the realm of adolescent dynamics is their increasing sensitivity to peer influence. Peers play a vital role during adolescence, often trumping family influence. The opinions and behaviors of their friends can significantly shape an adolescent's attitudes, values, and behaviour. This influence can lead to conflict with siblings, especially if they are not part of the same peer group.

So, how can parents navigate these unique dynamics to maintain and enhance sibling relationships? The first step is gaining a sense of perspective. Adolescence isn't the time for parents to panic, but a time to guide and support. There will be moments when it seems challenging, but the key is to remain consistent, patient, and understanding.

Promote open communication. Make it a point to talk with your teenagers about their feelings and thoughts. Having open-ended conversations can help them deal with their emotions better and also keep you updated about their lives. Remember, effective communication isn't just about talking, but listening too. By actively listening without judgment or immediate reactions, you're encouraging them to be more open and honest.

Strike a balance in freedom and restrictions. Teenagers crave independence, but they also require limits for safe exploration. It's important for parents to provide a balance where they feel trusted but also know there are boundaries that keep them safe. This sense of security and freedom can positively impact their relationship with siblings.

Foster respect and fairness in the household. One principle that should remain consistent from childhood to adulthood is respect. Adolescents should understand the importance of respecting their siblings' individuality, opinions, and space. Ensure that fairness prevails in the house and that privileges or penalties aren't doled out unjustly.

Encourage shared activities. Despite their quest for independence, adolescents still need a sense of belonging. Encourage siblings to participate in shared activities or have shared interests. There may be many differences surfacing at this stage, but finding common ground can help retain that sense of camaraderie and create lasting bonds.

Empathize with their struggles. Remember, adolescence can be an overwhelming phase. High school pressure, making career choices, navigating friendships - these can be quite a bit to deal with. Empathy goes a long way in helping them cope with these challenges and also fosters better sibling relationships.

Introduce positive role models. Teenagers often look up to and model their behavior after people they admire. If they see influential figures maintaining good relationships with their siblings, they might feel motivated to do the same.

Lastly, seek professional help when necessary. If sibling conflicts escalate or persist, it may be useful to involve a counselor or therapist. Sometimes, an external, neutral viewpoint can help resolve issues and provide strategies to maintain healthy relationships.

Remember, adolescence is not the end, but a transition. The key is understanding that adolescent dynamics are complex, variable, and influence the family, particularly sibling relationships. It's about steading the ship during the storm, not trying to stop the storm. With understanding, patience, and guidance, sibling bonds can continue to thrive in this phase of change and growth.

Preparing for the Challenges of Adulthood

Just as it was necessary to prepare your children for the transition into adolescence, you'll need to provide guidance as they edge closer to adult life. This part of the journey is every bit as challenging for parents as it is for the children themselves. So, let's delve into what these challenges might be and how to help your children overcome them.

You've fostered their sense of individuality and hopefully created an harmonious environment in your home. Still, adulthood is a different game altogether. It comes with responsibilities, independence, and freedom which can be overwhelming, particularly in sibling dynamics.

Firstly, it cannot be overstated how critical it is to instill in your children the value of strong work ethics. More than just a tool to earn a living, work is a substantial part of our adult identities. It encourages self-driven growth and individual responsibility. Encourage them to find what they enjoy and foster those passions into potential career paths. Ensure those conversations are a shared experience amongst siblings, inspiring mutual support in their pursuits.

Part of dealing with impending adulthood is growing with one's peer group. With a close-knit sibling group, there's a chance of social balkanization, where your children might form a social clique separate from their peers. Encouraging outward socializing and promoting friendships outside the family unit ensures a well-rounded social circle. It's important to discuss these concerns with your children and mobilize the siblings to support each other's social development.

Adulting, so to speak, can be an onslaught of responsibilities and decision-making. In the midst of it all, maintaining emotional health should be emphasized. It's not unusual for adults to neglect their emotional health when they're swamped with responsibilities. Teaching your children early about emotional autonomy and maturity can prevent distress later in life. Foster open conversations about feelings and emotions within your family and let siblings lean on each other during hard times.

Finances are a fundamental part of adulthood. And unfortunately, many young adults are ill-prepared to handle their finances as they step into the adult world. By introducing concepts of budgeting, spending, saving, and investing from a young age, you equip them with the knowledge they need. Encourage them to learn from each other's experiences with finances and remember, they're never too young to understand the value of a dollar.

Learning to care for themselves and their living environment is a crucial part of adulthood. Teach them the importance of cleanliness, healthy living, and discipline. Siblings can support each other here, maybe even making a friendly competition out of it.

Teaching problem-solving skills aren't just for conflict resolution. They're also a vital aspect of daily life. Foster independence by allowing your child to troubleshoot minor issues on their own. Remember to coach along the way to help them develop maturity in their decision-making processes.

Respect and kindness to all keep society functioning smoothly. Emphasize the virtue of basic common decency, not just towards siblings but also to people outside the family. As Martin Luther King Jr. said, "Kindness is a language the deaf can hear and the blind can see."

Practicing empathy and compassion brings a better understanding of people and situations. Encourage your children to take the perspective of their siblings, to allow forgiveness easier and resentment harder. Their relationship as siblings will be a microcosm of the relationships they'll foster in the future, so the more empathy they practice at home, the better they'll handle relationships outside.

Lastly, understand that adulthood isn't just about responsibilities and work, there's leisure and relaxation. Teach your children the importance of taking breaks and respecting their own time, as well as that of others. They should appreciate the downtime and learn how to balance work and play effectively.

Of course, while you teach them these skills and values, remember that learning and personal growth is a sophisticated process. They will struggle and even fail at times. As parents, your job is to facilitate, not dictate, their journey to adulthood.

Each child will face their own unique set of challenges on this journey. That's where a deep sibling relationship comes in handy. With the right guidance, these relationships can become an invaluable source of support and encouragement. Remember, you're not just raising children. You're nurturing the adults they'll become, with the relationships they'll carry into that adulthood.

The transition period to adulthood is a profoundly significant time that can either augment siblings' bonds or add friction to them. As you guide them along this path, remember the ultimate goal is to foster a lifelong friendship that will support them through the years. Your role doesn't stop once they become adults. As a parent, you continue to play an important role in nourishing this bond through your guidance and love.

Remember, adulthood will bring its share of trials and tribulations, but by fostering these skills, principles, and, most importantly, their sibling relationship, you've essentially equipped them with an in-built support system to weather any storm.

Maintaining Sibling Connections as Life Paths Diverge

As your children grow, they will begin to craft their unique paths in life. Each sibling will recognize their interests and develop personalities that may be diverse from one another. It's a significant milestone, celebrating independence, but it can pose a challenge to maintaining close sibling connections.

Inevitably, these individual pursuits might separate siblings physically, emotionally, or ideologically. Some might go off to college in different states, others might embark on careers that literally take them to different corners of the globe. Even within the same city, siblings can lead lives that don't overlap for days on end. This divergence is a normal part of growing up, but it doesn't mean siblings should lose touch.

Let's discuss some strategies to maintain sibling connections during these transformative years when paths start to diverge significantly.

First and foremost, it's crucial to remind your children that distance doesn't have to mean disconnection. In our era of advanced technology and easy travel, maintaining connection, even when physically far away, has never been easier. Regular video calls, emails, and even old-fashioned letters can keep siblings connected. Encouraging your children to share their experiences and make efforts to stay in touch can go a long way in preserving their bond.

Secondly, don't underestimate the power of commemorating shared experiences. Shared memories can become the foundation of sibling relationships in adulthood. Encourage your children to reminisce; it will provide them with a sense of unity and continuity.

You can further foster this connection by creating new traditions or continuing old ones. Whether it's a yearly family vacation or simply calling each other on birthdays, maintaining these traditions can keep siblings involved in each other's lives, and reinforce the idea that they are part of the same narrative, regardless of their diverging paths.

Another strategy is to encourage respect for each sibling's individual path. Sometimes, differences of opinion and lifestyle choices can create distance. It's essential to remind your children that they don't have to agree on everything to stay close. Supporting each other, even when they disagree, can actually strengthen their bond.

Universally, ensuring that you maintain an open door policy in your home can be a powerful enabler for sibling connection. By making sure your house remains a home for all of your children, no matter where their lives take them, you provide a common ground that sustains unity.

Aim to provide a listening ear and an encouraging word to each child, acting as a conduit between them. Share their news, their joys and struggles, with each sibling (within reason and respecting their privacy). Serving as a connecting link can foster a sense of shared lives and mutual concern among siblings.

It can be beneficial to get involved in each child's life as much as they will allow. Show interest in their activities, their friends, their hopes, and fears. This involvement will give you insight into their world, which, when shared with their siblings, can create tighter bonds.

Step back when needed, too. Allow space for your adult children to negotiate their relationships and dilemmas independently. Simultaneously, you should be available to offer support and guidance when they need it. Sometimes, the role of a parent in maintaining sibling connections is less about intervention and more about facilitating connection when needed.

Remember, each sibling relationship will look different, and that's okay. Just as each of your children is unique, so too will be their bonds with each other. Some may be best friends; others may be more distant but still caring. Understand that maintaining a connection doesn't mean forcing a certain type of relationship; it means keeping the lines of love, respect, and care open.

In conclusion, maintaining sibling connections as life paths diverge becomes easier when love, respect, and robust communication are encouraged. As a parent, you can be the essential bridge that brings these elements together, preserving the bonds between your children even as they craft their paths, their unique marks in the world.

Chapter 8: Special Scenarios in Siblinghood

Now we're stepping a bit off the beaten track to examine some special configurations of siblinghood. For many families, the term "sibling" stretches beyond the traditional connection of children born to the same parents. There's an increasing number of blended families today where step-siblings are introduced. This situation can sometimes be a bumpy road filled with trigger points surrounding acceptance, territory, and favoritism. It's crucial to help establish common ground, ensure every child feels valued, and build a sense of unity within the new family structure. Half-siblings might also be part of the family equation. Here, it's just as important to treat these relationships with intent and care, fostering shared experiences and preventing division. Lastly, let's not forget twins and multiples - a bundle of joy that carries a unique set of dynamics. The intrinsic bond between twins can make other siblings feel left out or pitched against a seemingly unbreakable team. Encourage individual relationships between twins and their siblings to prevent any feeling of exclusion. No matter the special scenario, keeping open lines of communication, treating each child as an individual with unique needs, and emphasizing mutual respect are always the most beneficial strategies.

Blended Families and the Introduction of Step-siblings

As we navigate the unique settings of siblinghood, it's crucial to recognize blended families and the introduction of step-siblings. This dynamic can present a specific set of challenges, but also beautiful opportunities to expand family bonds and enrich children's lives. The powerful connection between step-siblings can develop into valuable, lifelong bonds, just like those of biological siblings.

Blended families come into being due to various instances such as re-marriage, adoption, and fostering. Therefore, scenarios giving rise to step-siblings are diverse. Acceptance and other emotions come into play if one or both partners bring children into a new relationship. The transition requires sensitivity and a respectful approach from parents.

Introducing step-siblings begins with open, sincere communication. Discuss the concept of a blended family in child-friendly terms. Emphasize the aspects of gaining a bigger family and more people to care and love. It's essential to acknowledge their feelings, whether they convey excitement, fear, or uncertainty.

Remember, it's okay if the kids don't immediately become best friends. These relationships may take time to cultivate. But there are strategies and practices to create a harmonious environment and help foster these connections. Here are some helpful approaches to consider.

Strive for a fresh start in a new shared environment. If possible, consider moving into a new home where everyone can create fresh memories together. This helps to minimize feelings of invasion or territorialism that can occur when children feel their space has been "invaded" by newcomers.

If a move isn't practical, aim to create a neutral environment where each child has their personal space and a say in shared spaces. Providing an area where they can retreat to when they need alone time can be incredibly beneficial.

Promote understanding and empathy among step-siblings by encouraging discussions about feelings and experiences. Facilitate conversations where they can ask each other questions about their likes, dislikes, and what makes them comfortable or uncomfortable. This can help alleviate uncertainties and misconceptions.

Arranging family activities that require teamwork can also be beneficial. Such activities can orient children to work collaboratively instead of competitively. Over time, shared experiences and achievements foster camaraderie and mutual respect among step-siblings.

However, avoid forcing the relationships. Allow the relationships to develop naturally at their own pace. Some kids might take longer to warm up to the idea of having step-siblings or getting used to them. Patience will be your ally in this process.

Establishing a set of house rules everyone needs to follow is crucial. This not only promotes discipline but also ensures fairness. Equality among siblings, step or not, is key to avoiding feelings of favoritism or exclusion.

Recognize individuality and celebrate the unique qualities and achievements of each child. This helps in fostering individuality within the newly blended family unit. However, also balance this with group activities and recognize collective achievements that demonstrate the strength of working as a team.

Keep communication lanes open and encourage individual one-on-one time with each child. This keeps them from feeling overlooked amid the changes. They should know they can talk to you about their grievances, worries, and joys.

Blending a family is a journey that can be a beautiful, bonding experience, despite the challenges. Strong and validating step-sibling bonds can shape the foundation of the blended family unit. The journey might not always be smooth sailing, but with openness, patience, and empathy, you can navigate these unique dynamics successfully.

As a parent, you're also not alone in this endeavor. Engage the wider community, speak to others who've had similar experiences, and seek professional help if needed. Remember, it's your love and guidance that paves the way for fostering unity in diversity within your beautifully blended family.

Navigating Relationships with Half-siblings

After our discussions on the dynamics of sibling relationships, we'll now turn our attention specifically to the nuances of half-sibling relationships. Half-siblings share one biological parent, and while this doesn't make their relationships any less significant, it can introduce unique challenges and opportunities into sibling dynamics.

The first key to helping half-siblings forge strong bonds lies in open, honest communication. Acknowledge differences in family structures and emphasize the shared parentage as a connection. Avoiding the subject or shying away from questions can lead to confusion or resentment.

When children have a clear understanding of their family structure, they're less likely to feel insecure about their placement within the family. Ensure you are answering their questions about half-siblings genuinely and respectfully. If emotions arise, tackle them head-on, offering your comfort and understanding.

Ensure all your children, whole and half-siblings alike, are equally involved in your family activities. This shared time can bridge gaps and foster a feeling of belonging for all children. It's also an excellent opportunity for children to bond over shared experiences.

It's essential, too, to recognize the role of the other parent who isn't a common link in half-sibling relationships. Encourage relationships with non-common parents and step-siblings if that's feasible and safe. Maintain respectful conversations about the other parent, reiterating the importance of every family member.

If there is a significant age gap between half-siblings, you can frame this as an opportunity rather than a barrier. The older sibling can often play a nurturing role towards the younger one, helping them to develop empathy and caring skills.

Again, it may seem challenging when half-siblings aren't living in the same household. However, this doesn't mean that meaningful bonds can't form. Take advantage of technology, visits, joint vacations, and other shared experiences to foster connection.

Teach your children that they don't need to live together daily to love and support each other. Reinforce the concept that families can stay close despite distance or living arrangements. Regular communication, mutual respect, and affection can bridge these physical gaps.

Introducing a new sibling into the family already comes with an initial adjustment. If the sibling is a half-sibling, the process may take longer or include additional challenges. Let your child express their feelings freely and validate their emotions during this period.

Furthermore, remember to keep the environment as fair as possible. Avoid differentiating between whole and half-siblings in terms of privileges or expectations. When each child sees consistency in your behavior and expectations, they'll feel secure and loved.

Above all, emphasize the love that unites the family. Teach all your children, regardless of their biological connections, to appreciate their unique family situation. Every family is different, and each sibling relationship is a journey.

As a parent, facilitating and nurturing half-sibling relationships may initially seem complex. But by employing openness, understanding, and the principles we've discussed in earlier chapters, you can help your children connect on a deep level, regardless of how the family tree branches.

Remember, the strength of a family doesn't rest on biological connections alone but on the shared love, respect, and mutual support within the family. By guiding your children to understand and appreciate this, you're setting the foundation for a lifetime of loving, supportive sibling relationships.

Ultimately, whether your children are half-siblings, step-siblings, or full siblings, the goal is fostering relationships based on mutual respect, love, and understanding. Displaying these values in your interactions, communication, and problem-solving will aid your children in building strong, intimate, and lasting relationships with their siblings.

The Unique Dynamics of Twins and Multiples

The magic and mystery of twins and multiples have fascinated cultures around the world since ancient times. While all siblings share a unique dynamic, the relationship between twins and multiples often presents its own set of rewards and challenges that are worth exploring.

To begin, it's important to unravel the unique bond that twins and multiples often share. They've traveled the infancy journey together right from the womb. The simultaneous development often sparks an intense bond, an intuitive understanding, a shared language that even parents may struggle to decode. But as breathtaking as this connectedness can be, it can also lead to problems.

This unique bond can sometimes make twins and multiples overly reliant on each other. This form of dependency could hinder their ability to develop individual identities. It's essential to nurture each child's sense of self by acknowledging their individual achievements and fostering their unique interests.

One common concern that arises with twins and multiples is the issue of comparison. All siblings fall prey to comparison to a certain extent, but in the case of twins and multiples, the comparisons can get even more intense due to their shared age and experiences. Avoid comparing your children as much as possible. Instead, celebrate their individual accomplishments and make it clear that each child is special in their own way.

Another distinctive factor when dealing with twins or multiples is managing a sense of fairness. Twins or multiples often share everything from birthdays to clothes to toys, which can spark disputes. As a parent, it becomes essential to instil a sense of ownership while also encouraging sharing and cooperation.

Strengthening individuality within multiples is crucial. Encouraging separate friendships, allowing different after-school activities, or facilitating separate one-on-one time can help twins and multiples see themselves as independent beings. This doesn't mean they need to do everything separately, but providing opportunities for individual growth can aid in their personal development.

Just as twins can have a uniquely strong bond, they may also have pronounced rivalries. They are continually competing for the same resources - your time, attention, and affection. Recognizing their individual needs and ensuring that both feel equally loved and cherished can help reduce rivalries.

Twins and multiples often face unique social challenges as well. They may be viewed as a single unit in social situations or at school, despite having different personalities, talents, and interests. It's important to help them build their social skills both jointly and independently.

Twins can also experience pressure to stay at the same academic or development level. As parents, it's essential to let each twin learns and develops at their personal pace. Provide the resources and support they need individually, ensuring they are recognized for their individual abilities, not compared to their sibling.

Understanding and navigating the unique emotional landscape of twins and multiples is another key aspect. They often mirror each other's feelings or may react more intensely to the other's experiences due to their close connection. Acknowledge and discuss their feelings individually to understand their specific perspectives.

Apart from the challenges, remember that having twins and multiples is a unique joy. The shared experiences, mutual growth, and intimate understanding are rare gifts that not all siblings have. As parents, nurturing this special bond while cultivating individuality can empower your children to have a healthy, balanced relationship with each other.

The relationship dynamics of twins and multiples isn't always easy to understand, but by appreciating their individual personalities and acknowledging the unique bond they share, parents can help their children thrive independently while also relishing in the extraordinary connection that twins and multiples share.

In conclusion, dealing with twins and multiples requires a fine balance between cherishing their unique bond and nurturing their individual capacities. By understanding their unique dynamics, parents can ensure that they navigate the complexities effectively, fostering both sibling harmony and individual growth. Parenting twins and multiples might be a unique challenge, but with a little insight and a lot of love, it's a joy multiplied.

Chapter 9:
Building a Supportive Community

Coming off the heels of our examination of unique dynamics in the last chapter, it's evident how complex sibling relationships can be. Now, let's beam our focus on the broader community. A community can act as a safety net, providing the emotional and practical support that you and your children need. Your extended family, from grandparents to cousins and everyone in between, can enhance sibling relationships by offering additional layers of love, guidance, and insight. Those close-knit bonds within the family become a first line of defense against adversity. Outside your family, the circle of friends you cultivate can provide your children with alternate perspectives and values, further enriching their life experiences. These relationships can play a pivotal role in reinforcing your children's bonds with each other. Additionally, school and extracurricular activities are not just outlets for your kids to develop their interests but also an eco-system for them to learn about cooperation, responsibility, and empathy, traits that are invaluable in sibling interactions. It's essential to foster interactions that reflect the values and principles that your family holds dear. Remember, your children are always watching and learning from the environment around them. Building a supportive community sets up a mirror reflecting the strong sibling bonds you hope to establish and maintain within your family.

The Role of Extended Family in Sibling Relationships

Building a supportive community for your children extends beyond the confines of the immediate household. It includes grandparents, aunts, uncles, and cousins, essentially, the extended family, who can play a significant role in shaping sibling relationships. Their influences can indeed be powerful, especially considering that they typically have a wealth of experience and unique perspectives to offer.

The first point to consider is that extended family members can help reinforce family values. When siblings hear consistent messages about family expectations and morals from both parents and their extended family, it reinforces their significance. This shared understanding can help siblings unite around a common ethos, and foster more potent bonds.

Secondly, extended family often provides another layer of support. Grandparents, aunts, and uncles can offer additional care, love, and attention. These relationships can provide a rich source of comfort, reassurance, and guidance for siblings. As a result, they feel more secure and connected to their family, which can promote harmony and cooperation among siblings.

Extended family members can also offer valuable lessons on conflict resolution. It's no secret that siblings can have disagreements or disputes. Watching how their extended family handles conflicts and resolves differences can provide important learning opportunities. Siblings can adopt these strategies, leading to more peaceful resolutions when disagreements arise between them.

Moreover, extended family can often defuse sibling rivalries by offering neutral perspectives. They can step in as mediators during conflicts, providing balanced feedback that isn't tainted by daily interactions and biases, which is sometimes inevitable for parents. This impartial viewpoint can be enlightening for siblings and ease tension between them.

Extended family can also play an essential role in fostering individuality by recognizing and celebrating each child's unique attributes. When a child's attributes, skills, or interests are affirmed by extended family, the child's self-esteem is nourished. The child then feels more comfortable expressing his or her individuality within the sibling relationship, which results in a healthier dynamic.

By involving extended family in shared activities and traditions, you can create a sense of unity and belonging among siblings. Shared memories of family gatherings, holiday celebrations, or cultural rituals can help siblings bond closely. This sense of shared family history can build a strong foundation for sibling relationships, fostering mutual support and enduring affection.

The provision of additional adult role models is another great advantage. An uncle's resilience, a grandparent's wisdom, or an aunt's kindness can inspire siblings, providing multiple models of character traits and behaviors. This mosaic of influences can enrich sibling relationships by promoting respect, admiration, and love for each other.

In some instances, extended family members may offer opportunities for siblings to have individual experiences outside of their immediate family context. Staying with a grandparent or going on a trip with an aunt, for instance, can provide siblings with fresh perspectives and experiences, which they can then share with each other.

Extended family members can play a crucial role in mitigating the impact of stressful family situations. During times of upheaval or change, such as a move, illness, or a parent's job loss, the reassurance and support extended family members offer can provide a sense of stability, which is extremely beneficial for sibling relationships.

The digital age brings opportunities for siblings to connect with extended family members regardless of geographical distances. This connection can further strengthen sibling bonds as they share these distant relationships together.

However, it's important to respect and navigate family dynamics carefully. Not all extended family relationships are positive. There might be conflicts, resentments, or other troubling dynamics at play. It's crucial to guard your children against any negative influences or patterns of behavior.

At the end of the day, extended families have a rich potential for nurturing close, lasting bonds between siblings. They create a web of love, support, and shared experiences that can shape and enhance sibling relationships. As a parent, leveraging this network can add another layer to the robust support system that nurtures your children's relationship.

Remember, it's not about having a perfect family. It's about weaving together these various influences, experiences, and relationships into a supportive environment where siblings can grow, both individually and collectively. With your guidance, the influences of your extended family can profoundly enrich your children's sibling relationships.

Friendships that Enhance Family Bonds

Having recognized the significance of extended family in reinforcing sibling relationships, let's turn our attention to another crucial component of the wider social environment: friendships. Both the friendships that your children form independently and the shared companions your family enjoys can greatly enhance family bonds and promote harmonious sibling relationships.

Individually established friendships offer your children alternate perspectives and experiences. Broadening your children's horizons through friendships can help them appreciate, understand, and value their family relationships more. Furthermore, these external bonds help children experience different social dynamics, which can be translated into their sibling relationships and make them richer and deeper.

On the other hand, shared family friendships can help cultivate a sense of unity and collective identity. This includes shared experiences, collective memories, and mutual understandings. These shared bonds can enhance cohesion and a sense of belonging among siblings, which is an essential ingredient in fostering lifelong friendships between them.

So, the question that naturally arises is, how do we, as parents, help our children form these constructive friendships that enhance, and not hinder, family bonds? It might seem like a daunting task, especially with the extra challenges navigated in today's digital world. But don't worry, let's explore some practical steps you can take.

First, encourage your children to form friendships with individuals who share values similar to your family. Values are the bedrock on which relationships are built. By associating with friends who respect and appreciate the same principles, your children are likely to strengthen these beliefs and apply them to their sibling relationships.

Next, teach your children to respect differences. Diversity in friendships can enrich our lives and foster empathy. Encouraging your children to form friendships with people who have different backgrounds, experiences, or perspectives can teach them important lessons about acceptance and understanding, and these lessons can be very beneficial to sibling relationships.

Now, let's move on to shared family friendships. It can be a fine balance to strike, reminding children that while they may have separate circles of friends, shared family friends can create connections on a different level. Cultivate relationships with families who share similar interests or values; this can open up opportunities for shared activities that can bring siblings closer together.

It's also important to remember, as parents, we play a vital role in guiding our children's attitudes toward friendships. You can do this by model good, healthy friendships in your own life. Through your actions and interactions, you can teach your children valuable lessons about friendship - the give and take, the need for boundaries, and the importance of respect.

One more thing to consider is creating an inviting home environment. Aim to make your home a welcoming place where your children's friends want to hang out. This not only allows you to monitor their interactions better but also encourages shared experiences which strengthen family bonds.

Likewise, ensure your children feel safe discussing their friendships with you. Keep the lines of communication open and show genuine interest in their social lives. If they encounter issues or conflicts in their friendships, guide them towards a resolution, and draw parallels to potential situations they could face with their siblings.

Lastly, remember that quality trumps quantity when it comes to friendships. It's more important that your children have one or two truly good friends (both individual and shared) - friends who positively influence them and contribute to their lives - rather than a dozen or so 'casual' friends.

In this digital age, we can't forget the impact of online friendships. These can pose their own unique challenges for family dynamics. It's essential to educate your children about online safety, privacy, and the distinction between online and offline relationships, all of which we will discuss in detail in Chapter 12.

In conclusion, nurturing friendships that enhance family bonds is about equipping your children with the social skills they need to form healthy relationships, educating them about the value of these connections, and setting a good example through your relationships. With your guidance, these friendships can grow into a positive and powerful force that enhances the familial bonds between your children.

Being intentional in fostering these relationships will help your children learn how to navigate various social situations. Remember, as parents, we can guide and teach, but genuine friendships are a two-way street that involves choice, mutual respect, and shared experiences. So, encourage your children to invest time and energy in their friendships - after all, these friendships could end up being the secret ingredient to a stronger family and more harmonious sibling relationships.

School, Extracurriculars, and Sibling Interactions

After developing the foundation for strong sibling relationships at home, another critical place of interaction becomes more prominent in the children's lives – school. It is one considerable element that shapes sibling relationships in multiple ways. Let's start with the broader perspective first.

School is an environment that provides ample opportunities for interactions and collaborations between siblings. When siblings attend the same school, the bond between them often strengthens, since they navigate common settings and shared experiences.

However, they might also face school-related competition, such as academic comparison and contrasting performances in different areas, like sports, arts, and extracurricular activities. It's crucial as parents to reassure them that their achievements are not relative to their siblings, and individual capabilities and strengths vary.

Siblings might have different inclinations and strengths, and it's essential to remind them that comparison does no good. Instead, focusing on their own growth will bring much more joy and satisfaction. This reassures your children that they are loved and valued for who they are, not how they perform relative to their siblings.

Speaking of performance, extracurricular activities can significantly influence sibling relations. Activities outside of regular school hours offer siblings additional avenues to bond over shared interests, pave the way for mutual support, or even ignite healthy rivalry.

If siblings are involved in the same extracurricular activities, they find more common ground, ample opportunities to interact, and shared experiences. This can strengthen their bond, promote mutual respect, and develop camaraderie. It is also beneficial for older siblings to guide and support younger siblings in understanding the nuances of the activity better.

On the flip side, if each child prefers different activities, it gives them a chance to establish their own identities. This helps each child feel special and avoid unnecessary comparisons. It also provides a platform for siblings to learn from each other's experiences by sharing individual learnings and accomplishments.

An additional element of sibling interaction in schools and extra-curricular activities is peer influence. It might be that friends from their respective age groups affect their relationships. It's a good idea to talk to your children about this and remind them not to let external influences affect their bond.

School also brings occasions like parent-teacher meetings, school plays, sports day, where families participate together. These instances can strengthen sibling bonds where they support each other, be proud of each other's achievements, and comfort each other when things don't go as planned.

However, let's not overlook that school is also where competition between siblings most likely gets heightened. Here, parents need to take particular care to avoid unhealthy competition, defuse tension, and foster positive interactions.

It's critical to foster a culture of healthy rivalry where siblings can compete, challenge, and push each other without crossing a certain line. This will not only support their individual growth but also strengthen their bond.

Similarly, in extracurricular activities, healthy competition among siblings can stimulate personal growth. However, parents need to keep an eye on the nature of this competition to prevent any harm to their relationship.

Sibling relationships are intertwined with their school lives and extracurricular activities, where they learn teamwork, rivalry, competition, cooperation, and mutual respect for the first time - on their home ground. So, while one might think that school and extra-curricular activities are exclusively about individual growth, we can see that they play a critical role in shaping sibling relationships.

Remember, fostering these relationships requires continuity and consistency.

Chapter 10:
Stories from the Trenches

In this chapter, we delve into the heart of real-life families, presenting stories that reveal challenges and triumphs in the realm of sibling relationships. These testimonies cut across various experiences, capturing unique moments of sibling rivalry, reconciliation, growth, and connections. Expect to find resonating scenarios, and perhaps a glimpse of your family reflected in the experiences of others. Woven in between these narratives are insightful interviews with child psychologists and counselors, providing expert insight into situations, reactions, and the underlying dynamics at play. Through this combined approach, we'll navigate raw emotions, secret battles, whispered apologies, and triumphant reconciliations, all reflecting the multi-layered complexity of sibling relationships. It's like we're getting a front row seat to witness the high and lows of the sibling journey, and in the process, gaining understanding and practical guidance for our own path.

Real-life Testimonials of Challenges and Triumphs

While understanding siblinghood from a theoretical viewpoint is beneficial, no tool offers straight-to-heart insights like real-life experiences. For many parents, nothing is more relatable—and, often, more inspiring—than hearing about the challenges and victories faced by fellow parents. This section offers the opportunity do so.

Let's start with Anna, a mother of three. Anna's biggest challenge was transforming the constant rivalry among her children into mutual respect. She started by recognizing each child's unique abilities, thus lessening comparison. The result wasn't immediate, but gradually, the siblings began to appreciate each other's specialties, making their relationships stronger.

We also spoke to Tom, a single father who was deeply concerned about the widening gap between his two teenage sons. Tom decided to address the issue by creating a safe space for open dialogue, endeavoring to encourage his sons to express their feelings. His tactic was a success—his sons began to understand each other's viewpoints better and their relationship improved significantly.

Dana's story offers another perspective. With two young daughters close in age, she had to manage constant competition and petty arguments. Her strategy was to introduce collaborative activities that necessitated mutual cooperation. Developing a sense of teamwork not only reduced disputes, but also fostered a deep bond between her daughters.

When it comes to overcoming challenges, Samantha's plight stands out. She was tasked with navigating relationships between her son and newly introduced step-siblings after marrying her second husband. The initial period was full of hurdles—resentment, jealousy, and a sense of insecurity. With patience, she gradually broke down barriers, assuring her son of his importance in her life, while also emphasizing the importance of his new family. Her unwavering effort led to successfully blending the family.

Mark, a father of twins, shares how he handled the innate competition between them. His approach was to highlight their unique qualities without comparison, ensuring equal focus and appreciation for both twins. This approach led them to be comfortable with their identities, reducing rivalry significantly.

Sonia, a mother struggling with her children's extreme age gaps, realized she had to devise strategies tailored to her unique family structure. Sonia encouraged bonding over shared family memories and experiences and facilitated understanding about different life stages. By doing so, she was able to build a strong connection between her children despite their age difference.

Then there's Kevin, who was having difficulty balancing individual time and group activities with his children. He started giving each child one-on-one time, focusing on their interests. He also organized group activities that everyone could enjoy. This approach led to a happier dynamic among his children who felt individually valued and also part of the group.

Jane was worried when her kids started to drift apart after stepping into adulthood. She reminded them of the crucial role they played in each other's lives by encouraging regular sibling hangouts and family get-togethers. Over time, Jane was relieved to see the siblings maintain their bond even as they pursued their individual life paths.

Finally, we have Lily, a mother who managed to harness the power of her community to enhance her children's sibling bonds. She used extended family interactions and friendships to foster a sense of togetherness among her children. She found her children's bonds became stronger when they understood they were part of a larger nurturing environment.

These stories offer valuable insights into the methods that different parents applied to address their unique challenges.

Not all strategies may work for every family due to various factors such as family structure, personalities of children, and external influences. However, they serve as inspirations to devise your strategies and to forge ahead in the journey of fostering healthy sibling relationships.

In conclusion, it's clear that the path to fostering healthy sibling relationships can be filled with trials. However, triumph can be achieved by using practical and personalized strategies. It isn't necessarily about finding a perfect solution instantly, rather, it's about the consistent effort to engage in a loving, compassionate, and understanding approach.

Whether you're dealing with sibling rivalry, developmental differences, teenage dynamics, or any other unique scenario, remember that the journey is steeped with learning experiences not just for your children, but for you as well. It's through these challenges that resilience and understanding are built, ultimately enhancing the sibling bond within your family.

We hope these testimonials have provided you with some encouragement and inspiration. Remember that although the road can be challenging, fostering harmonious sibling relationships is not only doable but can also be exceptionally rewarding. It's these bonds that, once cultivated and nurtured, become a source of lifelong support, companionship, and love.

Expert Insights: Interviews with Child Psychologists and Counselors

We've discussed the nuances of sibling relationships from historical, psychological, and practical perspectives. Now, let's delve into the insights of professionals who work with children and their families daily. These are experienced child psychologists and counselors who have lent their expertise to our understanding of sibling dynamics.

The first interview is with a child psychologist who emphasizes the significance of understanding the individual needs of each child. "Every child is unique, and dealing with siblings requires an approach sensitive to each child's individuality. Recognizing their strength and fostering a positive identity can help in reducing rivalry," she affirms.

Another expert, a child counselor, shares how parents can mediate disputes between siblings positively. He believes that parents can help siblings see conflicts as an opportunity for mutual growth rather than a win-or-lose situation. "Guiding them to resolve disputes with compassion and understanding can cement their bonds," he asserts.

A renowned psychologist underlines the power of positive reinforcement in sibling relationships. "When a child sees their sibling receiving praise for good behavior, they'll be inherently motivated to act similarly," she explains. According to her, encouraging sibling unity while respecting individual preferences fosters a healthier bond.

Sharing insights on the role of parents, an experienced counselor states, "Parents are like coaches. They aren't just observers but active participants in shaping the sibling dynamics. They can introduce healthy competition, ensure fair play, and encourage mutual respect in their children."

One child psychologist discusses the importance of parents examining their own attitudes. "It's essential that parents introspect and identify if they are unconsciously favoring one child over the other. Even a subtle bias can sow the seeds of rivalry," he warns.

Discussing the unique dynamics of blended families or those with half-siblings and step-siblings, a family therapist advises, "Patience, understanding, and proactive communication are key. Creating a culture of inclusivity and belongingness can be pivotal in blending families."

When asked about addressing common triggers of sibling rivalry, a counselor specialising in children's and teenagers' mental health suggests, "Understanding the roots of rivalry can help in pinpointing triggers. Teaching children empathy and taking time for individual attention can alleviate feelings of envy and competition."

A psychologist specializing in the area of adolescent dynamics points out the role of peer influence. "Teenagers often compare themselves with their social group, and siblings are usually the first on the list. Educating them about the futility of comparison and promoting self-acceptance is crucial during this stage," she advises.

We also have experts weighing in on how modern challenges affect sibling relationships. A counselor who regularly deals with issues around social media and online gaming says, "Digital platforms can either foster stronger bonds or generate more conflict, depending on how they're used. Parents need to foster a healthy digital culture at home."

Lastly, a child psychologist emphasizes the importance of raising resilient children. "Resilience is not just about weathering hardships, but also about leaning on each other for support. Siblings can play a significant role in building each other's resilience," she concludes.

The crux of these expert insights points us towards understanding, empathy, fair play, effective communication, appreciation of individuality, fostering positivity, and building resilience as indispensable tools in shaping sibling relationships. It's a delicate balance, but, when achieved, it can lay the foundation for sibling bonds that endure a lifetime.

Chapter 11:
Building Resilience Through Sibling Bonds

Let's now pivot to explore how sibling bonds contribute to building resilience in children. Throughout life's rollercoaster of ups and downs, siblings can serve as powerful allies, offering emotional security and support during times of adversity. Siblings often form a child's first peer group, and their interactions—rich in disputes, camaraderie, and lessons learnt—can infuse them with vital soft skills such as conflict resolution, compromise, and empathy. These competencies not only bolster resilience but also prove invaluable in future encounters beyond the home—whether it's negotiating at school, navigating friendships, or coexisting at the workplace. However, this resilience-building aspect of the sibling relationship doesn't just spontaneously emerge; it requires nurturing. It's imperative to foster environments where siblings feel safe to express their feelings and experiences. Encourage open dialogue and strengthen these bonds by demanding fairness, modeling respect, and celebrating their unique qualities. Remember, when children know they have a steadfast supporter in their sibling, they're more likely to bounce back from life's challenges and less likely to feel isolated or overwhelmed. Essentially, what we are discussing here is not just resilience, but the power of family.

The Role of Siblings in Facing Adversities

Having spent the past chapters delving into the unique dynamics, conflicts, and rewards of sibling relationships, we now find ourselves at a point where we need to address the role of sibling bonds when it comes to facing adversities. Life cannot always be a smooth sail, and in those periods of stormy weather, the strength of sibling ties can prove invaluable.

It's crucial to understand that when children face adversities, they don't just want an adult's hand to hold – they are equally comforted by the companionship of their siblings as well. In essence, siblings act as each other's safety nets, their beacons guiding them through the foggy paths of hardship.

Hardships are inevitable in life, but within the realms of adversity are hidden opportunities for children to bond deeply, sharpen their problem-solving skills, understand empathy, exercise resilience, and fulfill their roles as supporters, comforters, and inspirers—even when the person in need is as familiar as their own sibling.

But how is this relationship developed? One key ingredient is time. Time spent together during both joyous and challenging times fosters an environment of shared experiences that siblings can lean on during trying periods. This, coupled with the shared history and insider knowledge only siblings possess, can forge bonds that are largely unshakeable.

For you as parents, the way you model resilience and strength in the face of difficulties plays a significant role in how your children will react. If you show them that it's okay to ask for help and lean on each other, they'll feel more comfortable doing it too.

Encourage them to communicate and express their thoughts and feelings, not just in times of happiness, but also during times of distress. Make it a family practice to discuss problems and seek solutions together. This won't just bring the siblings closer, but it will also provide them with the ability to problem-solve, a skill that is critical in all walks of life.

Another key way to bolster the sibling support system is to inculcate the value of empathy. Empathy is not a trait that children are born with—it's something they learn and grow into. As parents, it's your job to show them what empathy looks like through your own actions and reinforce its importance in building strong relationships.

Remember, your goal is not to eradicate adversity— a feat that's not only impossible but also unnecessary. In the grand scheme of their lives, these trials and tribulations will serve as stepping stones towards building resilience. Instead, your focus should be on equipping them with the abilities to confidently wade through turbulent times while reminding them of the sibling net always present to catch them when they fall.

Be mindful not to inadvertently foster a hyper-dependency during these times, though. While it's excellent for siblings to be each other's support network, don't lose sight of the fact that each child is an individual who needs to develop their coping mechanisms. The goal is a balanced mix of familial support and personal resilience —not a crutch that hampers the development of self-reliance.

Your role also doesn't end after setting this sibling-support system in motion. It'll require your ongoing effort to ensure that each child feels heard, understood, and loved within this support system. Regular check-ins and open-ended conversations about their feelings can ensure that their bond remains a source of comfort rather than an added pressure.

To sum up, the adversities siblings face together can be potent catalysts for bonding tightly and growing personally. Through shared adversity, siblings can see each other in new roles: as guardians, cheerleaders, and devoted allies. This new perspective can add layers of depth to their relationship that don't just make it stronger but also more mature.

In the end, remember, as a parent, you don't have to have all the answers or solutions to their problems. What's crucial is that you create an environment where siblings feel safe to express their vulnerabilities and are empowered to seek and find power in their collective strength. In doing so, you set them up for a lifetime of healthy problem-solving and solid resilience.

As we move forward, we will explore ways siblings can support each other through life's ups and downs and delve into the powerful lessons in resilience these experiences reveal, ensuring that the bonds of siblinghood are a support system your children can rely on throughout their lives.

Supporting Each Other Through Life's Ups and Downs

The bond between siblings is a lifeline, especially during life's harder moments. To help your children extend their support to each other through thick and thin, it's crucial that you empower them first with emotional resilience and the knowledge that they can confide in and depend on each other. This chapter dives deep into developing these skills.

The process begins with cultivating empathy. Encourage your children to put themselves in their sibling's shoes. This doesn't mean they need to agree with each other all the time, but understanding and acknowledging their feelings is a language that says 'I'm here for you' without words and forms the basis of emotional support.

Teach your children the importance of listening to each other's problems without dismissing them. Sometimes, a good listener is what we need more than advice. Reassure them that it's okay to not have all the answers and that simply being a shoulder to lean on can be powerful.

It's also essential to provide a stable, supportive environment at home, where every family member feels free to express their feelings without fear of being judged or ridiculed. This not only boosts their confidence but also creates a setting where emotional support thrives, planting the seeds for supportive sibling relationships.

While ups and downs are inevitable, focus on modeling strategies for managing these phases effectively. Highlight the importance of staying calm, not dwelling on negative aspects, and focusing on solutions rather than problems. Teaching these coping skills can equip your children to handle challenges together and emerge stronger.

Developing the skill of collaborative problem-solving is another essential aspect. When siblings face a joint problem, guide them to brainstorm possible solutions together, weigh the pros and cons, and reach a consensus. This interaction not only helps them address the issue at hand but also strengthens their bond.

On the journey of life, siblings may face personal challenges such as academic pressures, social worries, or health issues. In such situations, providing opportunities for them to converse openly about these difficulties can help them see each other as allies rather than competition, fostering mutual support.

Don't forget to celebrate the victories along the way, big or small. Use these occasions to reinforce the importance of being there for each other, not just during struggles but in triumphs as well. Encourage your children to recognize and applaud each other's achievements, fortifying their unique bond.

Remember, it's normal for siblings to have misunderstandings or disagreements. However, it's crucial to guide them to resolve these conflicts amicably, not letting such incidents strain their relationship. Turn these squabbles into teachable moments, imparting the valuable lesson of forgiving and moving forward.

Lead by example. Show your children that as parents, you're there for them unconditionally. Let them see that even adults need support and have their own ups and downs, reinforcing that everyone benefits from emotional support.

Often, your children might find it hard to express their feelings in words. Encourage them to use creative outlets like art, music, or storytelling to discuss their emotions. This not only helps them communicate more effectively but also boosts their emotional intelligence, equipping them to understand and support each other better.

Acknowledge your children's efforts to support each other. Positive reinforcement inspires them to continue these behaviors. However, be careful not to compare them or favor one over the other, as this can negatively impact their relationship.

Finally, remind your children that it's okay to ask for help when they need it. While self-reliance is essential, knowing that it's normal to need others, especially during hard times, is just as important. This understanding can enhance their ability to seek and provide support in their sibling bonds.

Remember, the process of developing a supportive network between your children isn't a sprint—it's a marathon. The investment in encouraging and guiding your children to be there for each other can strengthen their bond, setting them up for a supportive and unified relationship through life's inevitable ups and downs.

Lessons in Resilience and the Power of Family

This chapter aims to delve into the profound impact that families—it's strength, unity, and love—can have in fostering resilience. We will explore the gritty and wonderful lessons that family dynamics and sibling relationships can provide when weathering hardships and adversities.

Resilience is the ability to recover from difficulties. It's about bouncing back from challenges and growing stronger in the process. It's an essential life skill that's nurtured over time. It doesn't evolve in isolation.

Studies reveal that family plays a substantial role in building resilience among children. The strength of the relationships they establish within their family structure, their interaction with their siblings, and the support they receive all factor into resilience development.

Resilience can often be misinterpreted as a trait that people are born with. The reality is that resilience is shaped over time and influenced by a person's environment. The family, being a child's foremost ecosystem, plays a significant role in sculpting a child's resilience.

Every family faces challenges—stress, loss, illnesses, to name a few—but how a family emerges from such trials mostly depends on an intricate balance of support, communication, and a shared understanding of the issue.

When siblings navigate these adversities together, it fosters a special bond and interdependence that builds resilience. They learn to share disappointment and joy, giving them a glimpse into the inevitable ups and downs in life. And this becomes a precursor to cultivating resilience.

This sharing within families tends to help children see that they're not alone in their struggles. Their siblings are usually there alongside them, going through the same trials. This sense of shared experiences forms a strong safety net, teaching them the value of collective resilience.

Siblings' resilience is often intertwined—their collective strength in facing adversities is embedded in their shared experiences and commitment to mutual support. Interactions and relationships within families, particularly between siblings, provide an excellent platform for children to learn and nurture resilience.

Communication and support are key facets of family resilience. Family strengths such as belief systems, organizational patterns, and open communication nurture resilience and cultivate a rich environment for children to understand adversity and cope with it.

When parents encourage open communication while navigating trials, children are more likely to learn essential problem-solving skills. These skills are fortified when siblings also partake in open conversations about the challenges they face within and outside the family structure.

The strength within families doesn't always originate from being immune to conflict or stress. Instead, it often develops from successful navigation, confrontations, and resolutions of these inevitable family obstacles. It's the constant ebb and flow of conflicts and resolutions that offers the wealth of lessons families bring to the table.

The family unit's efficacy is built upon mutual respect, shared understanding, inclusive decision-making, and fair dealing with each other. Parents who model such behavior lay the groundwork for their children's resilience-building.

Moreover, parents' acknowledgment of each child's unique ability and individuality promotes self-confidence and respect for differences, which are essential for resilience as it helps the child value and believe in themselves despite adversities.

This chapter, therefore, emphasizes that resilience isn't a solitary endeavor. The family, with all its intricate dynamics and varying personalities, functions as a resilience-building powerhouse. Its collective strength and unity often serve as the bedrock for a child's ability to cope, persevere, and thrive amid life's challenges.

In the end, it's important to comprehend that family and resilience go hand in hand. We just need to unlock that potential. Let's unlock that potential together.

Chapter 12: Navigating Modern Challenges

As we move forward into the digital era, the dynamic of sibling relationships inevitably has to adapt. The influx of technological advancements such as social media and online gaming platforms poses new challenges. As parents, understanding our children's digital lives can feel daunting, but it's crucial to their safety and wellbeing. It's not about restricting their exposure, but guiding them to use these platforms conscientiously to foster healthier sibling relationships. Similarly, modern pressures surrounding school work, peer influence, and societal expectations require us to be vigilant, supportive, and proactive. Open dialogue about these topics, paired with stress management techniques can help alleviate anxieties your children may face. Change, while often overwhelming, signifies growth. So, as families in the 21st century, adapting to these changes involves not only understanding the environment your children are now growing up in but reinventing our parenting strategies to better equip them for the challenges ahead. And remember, throughout this modern maze, the core principles of love, respect, and understanding within family units remain central to fostering long-lasting sibling bonds.

The Digital Age: Social Media, Gaming, and Sibling Relations

We're now walking into a distinct era where our children are gradually immersed in digital platforms. This age of progression brings about unique challenges and opportunities concerning sibling relationships. We're going to look at the impact of social media, online gaming and how we can facilitate positive sibling relations amidst all this.

First, on social media. Displayed as an accessible platform where kids keep touch with friends, follow their interests, express themselves or simply pass time, social media undoubtedly plays a significant role in their social development. But like everything else, it comes with its benefits and drawbacks.

Social media can be an opportunity for siblings to bond. They might share viral videos, tag each other in memes, share an account on Instagram for their pet or even start their YouTube channel. Encourage such fruitful collaboration; it cultivates shared interests, teamwork, communication and respect for each other's inputs.

Some challenges, however, might spring forth. Siblings can encounter conflicts online—unwanted tags in unflattering photos, embarrassing comments or more serious issues involving privacy breaches. Here, it's crucial to cultivate an understanding of mutual respect and boundaries in the digital space, akin to the physical world.

Getting into gaming, another favorite digital pastime, we see it has equally transformative power in the dynamic between siblings. Co-operative games can set the stage for siblings to work as a team, while healthy competitive games can help them understand winning, losing and fair play.

Some kids, not being equal in their gaming skills, might face conflicts. The older one might hog the game, or the younger one might feel left out because they're not as competent. Here's where you can step in, ensuring everyone gets enough turns, and helping them appreciate each other's gaming style and skills.

Role-playing, strategy or creative games can also foster creativity, leadership skills, problem-solving and negotiation skills. The siblings learn to strategize, negotiate, divide roles, and appreciate the sense of achievement when they succeed together.

However, conflicts among siblings over screen time, the content of games, or testing their limits can't be overlooked. Like the case with social media, reinforcing respect, sharing and understanding in gaming is paramount.

Now, intertwining digital tools with sibling dynamics isn't about letting the tech do all the work but understanding and harnessing its potential while limiting the drawbacks. Here's a few ways to do this:

- *Set Clear Boundaries:* Put up reasonable time limits for the usage of digital platforms. Too much of anything isn't good, even if it's proving to be a bonding tool for your kids.

- *Ensure Privacy:* Teach your kids about the importance of privacy online, ensuring they understand not to share personal details or photos of their siblings without consent.

- *Promote Positive Interaction:* Encourage your kids to share interesting finds or engage in activities online that fuse their relationship.

Digital Literacy: Talk about the responsible use of social media and games, such as respecting others online, understanding that winning isn't everything, and acknowledging that people can be different offline.

Remember, the digital space can offer a unique avenue for siblings to interact, understand each other and build a bond. But, just like in the physical world, your guidance is essential in navigating this digital world, replete with both opportunities and challenges.

Let's embrace digital platforms as tools than view them as barriers. Through understanding and balance, we can indeed foster a positive sibling relationship in this digital era. The idea is to use them as a means to uplift the essence of siblinghood, not replace it.

Modern-Day Pressures: School, Peer Influence, and Expectations

After considering the role of the digital age in sibling relationships, it's time to focus on other pertinent pressures that your children might encounter. In our modern society, the domains of school, peer influence, and expectations weigh heavily on a child's psyche, consequently affecting their familial and sibling relationships.

Firstly, let's talk about school. It's a microcosm of the real world - it's where your children start to step out of the familial nest and test their social skills. There's no doubt that school pressure can significantly impact the relationship between siblings. Competition may arise, especially if siblings are close in age or in the same educational institution. While competition can promote growth, it can also cause strain in their relationship when unchecked.

The key to managing this pressure is to cultivate a home environment that values support over competition. Ensure your children understand that their individual efforts and improvements are doors to success, and not necessarily how they perform in comparison to their siblings. Encourage them to help each other in academics - let older siblings tutor the younger ones when they can, fostering support and camaraderie.

On the other hand, peer influence is a dual-edged sword. It can motivate children to better themselves, or it can contribute to feelings of inadequacy and stress. Past the immediate household, peers often represent a significant proportion of a child's world. As such, it's necessary to acknowledge this powerful influence over your children.

Now, remember, you can't handpick your children's friends, but you can instill values that will help them choose their friends wisely. Additionally, encouraging open dialogue about their social interactions helps you guide them through challenging situations or influences. Understanding their social circle also enables you to discern how it affects their sibling dynamics.

Under peer influence, siblings may either bond together as allies against external social pressures or be driven apart by differing social experiences. Again, nurturing a supportive family atmosphere with open communication lines serves as an excellent strategy to leverage peer influence positively. This cooperation will fortify their resilience in the face of negative peer pressure.

Lastly, expectations, both perceived and real, are far-reaching pressures that influence our children. In their pursuit to excel - whether in academics, sports, arts, or other fields - they might feel the weight of expectations intensifying, much more so when these are expectations they believe their parents have set. When dealing with siblings, these expectations can multiply; comparisons can occur, fostering a sense of rivalry or even resentment.

As parents, it's your role to clearly communicate your expectations - taking care not to set the bar too high nor too low. More importantly, these expectations should focus on their effort, progress, and integrity instead of just outcomes and achievements. Reinforce the idea that you love and appreciate them for who they are and not what they accomplish. Cultivate an environment of respect where each child feels valued and understood in their uniqueness.

Seeing their parents handle expectations impartially can neutralize rivalry among siblings. Let your children understand that while their journeys might differ, each path is equally valuable. Do not allow achievements in one area to overshadow successes in other fields. You want every child, regardless of their distinct talents or strengths, to feel equally cherished.

Every child's journey is unique, and so is their relationship with their siblings. The pressures of school, peers, and expectations are real and powerful, but they can also be incredible opportunities for growth. They can become the milieu where your children learn essential values and life skills that even the best curriculum can't provide. But, as with everything, these opportunities require nurturing - something that begins at home, excellently guided by conscientious parenting.

Undoubtedly, modern pressures can push siblings apart if left unchecked. However, the same pressures can serve as the soil in which the seeds of a steady and supportive sibling bond can grow and flourish. This journey is not without its challenges, but remember, as parents, you're adequately equipped to guide and help your children navigate through these pressures together. And in doing so, solidify the bond they share, leaving them with an irreplaceable gift - a lifetime of friendship with their siblings.

Adapting to Change: Strategies for the 21st-Century Family

The ever-evolving twenty-first-century landscape presents unique challenges to families, requiring adaptations in parenting and the overall functioning of the family unit. The ubiquity of technology, new types of family structures, global social challenges, and swiftly changing societal norms require families to find strategies to adapt and thrive.

At the heart of this adaptability lies the ability to embrace change rather than fighting or denying it. It's essential to understand that evolution is a part of life and that our aim should be to navigate it effectively as a family, creating a supportive, tolerant, and accepting environment for everyone.

Imparting soft skills to children that foster resilience, empathy, and open-mindedness is a vital part of this journey. Skills such as problem-solving, interpersonal communication, and critical thinking help children adapt to change seamlessly. Fostering emotional intelligence aids children in understanding not just their own feelings, but also those of others around them.

As a family unit, embracing change can be achieved by prioritizing clear and effective communication. This involves open family discussions about changes and the emotions associated with them, teaching children to adapt by incorporating their views. Remember that children are resilient, and when we let them express themselves freely, they adapt better.

With an increase in diverse family structures, including single parents, blended families, multigenerational living, and families with LGBTQ+ parents, celebrating diversity and promoting inclusivity is integral. Demonstrating acceptance and appreciation for all forms of life and love will instill these values in your children as well.

In this digital era, one can't ignore the significant role technology plays. While it has its advantages, it also poses risks to the mental health and safety of children. It's critical to maintain open dialogue about digital safety: this includes discussions on cyberbullying, online privacy, and the time spent on digital devices, among others.

Moreover, recognizing that every child is different and encouraging them to embrace their individuality is pivotal. As they grow, provide them with space to explore their identities, supporting them in their exploration, preparing them for the various challenges they might face, and standing by their choices.

Education is a significant part of adapting to change. Encourage your children to think globally and act locally. Empower them to be part of the solution to issues affecting the world, teach them to respect and appreciate cultural, racial, and individual differences, and foster a sense of responsibility for the planet.

The rapid pace of modern life can leave little time for rest and relaxation, leading to high-stress levels. Teach your children effective stress management techniques and ensure some downtime in their daily schedules. Balance in life is key.

Time is the biggest gift you can give your family. Despite the hustle and bustle of modern life, ensure that you spend quality time as a family. Family rituals, shared meals, and vacations help build a strong family connection that provides a secure base for children to explore their world and adapt to changes.

The role that parents play in modelling behavior cannot be overstated. Your responses to changes greatly influence how your children perceive and respond to changes. Therefore, demonstrate resilience, compassion, and open-mindedness amidst changes.

In this rapidly evolving world, it's more about shaping the values that will help your children navigate their paths with courage, kindness, and resilience. The essential attributes parents can shape within their children are adaptability, resilience, and a world-ready attitude.

Remember, the goal isn't to shield our children from change or to eliminate the challenges they will face. Instead, we should aim to equip them with the right tools, attitudes, and beliefs to navigate their course successfully. By using opportunities for growth that arise within the family, you can foster an environment that prepares your child for a continually changing world.

By adopting these strategies, you enable your family to adapt to the 21st-century changes with optimism and resilience, supported by empathetic bonds of siblinghood. Growth and adaptation are parallel paths in this journey of life; with open conversations and supportive guidance, you can ensure that every family member is prepared to face, understand, and embrace the winds of change positively.

Conclusion

And so our journey comes to a close. As your family navigates the complexities of sibling bonds, remember that every little step counts. Regardless of the highs and lows, the petty fights or profound moments of affection, what you're really fostering is a lifelong relationship that can bring immeasurable joy and shared strength. Embrace the inevitable ups and downs of parenthood, resilient in the knowledge that the effort you put in today will become tomorrow's bond, built upon mutual respect, individuality within unity, and the shared memories that form the foundation of familial affection. Looking ahead, envision a home filled with the inviting sound of friendly family bonds, as exciting and unpredictable as your kids themselves. This isn't merely about avoiding squabbles or managing rivalry. It's about guiding your children towards understanding, empathy, and the genuine love that siblings can share. And remember, there's no definitive guide to parenting – so take every advice as a direction, not an absolute. The beauty of this journey lies in its uniqueness. Align your strategies with your family's character and trust your instincts—you've got this.

Embracing the Journey of Parenthood

Parenting isn't just a role; it's a journey full of beautiful, humorous, heartbreaking, and enlightening moments. It's a formidable voyage that transforms us in countless ways. At the heart of this transformation is an understanding and appreciation of the difference we can make in our children's lives and the powerful bonds we can help them form with their siblings.

For many, the journey of parenting unravels haphazardly like a ball of yarn. One season of life flows into the next, leaving behind a trail of lessons learned, mistakes made, and victories celebrated. This is simply the nature of parenthood - it's a constant learning experience and calls for a level of patience, wisdom, and understanding that most of us didn't know we had.

Remember that parenting, like any journey, has its highs and lows. There will be times of joy and laughter, as well as times of frustration and confounding questions. It's crucial to approach parenting with an open mind and heart, ready to experience and learn from every situation. No two days will be the same, and that's what makes this journey so rewarding and significant.

There's no such thing as a perfect parent. We all, without exception, make mistakes and have room to grow. The goal isn't to parent flawlessly but to love and guide our children unconditionally. Keep in mind that you are doing your best, and that's more than enough. Accept your limitations, forgive yourself, and use each day as an opportunity to grow alongside your children.

One key facet of the parenting journey is fostering a strong bond between siblings. From the moment a new baby joins the family, it's essential to nurture the relationship between your children. Encourage your older child to interact with their younger sibling, help them understand the baby's needs, and reassure them of your unwavering love.

As your children grow older, steer them towards a stronger bond with their siblings. Teach them the importance of family, the beauty of unconditional love, and the power of togetherness. Amidst the everyday chaos, create space for shared experiences that help your children create lasting memories.

Encourage their individuality while cultivating mutual respect. This isn't always easy in a world that naturally spurs comparison and competition. But when your children know that they're valued for who they are and not compared against their sibling, it fosters a healthier family dynamic.

Remember, your children's relationship will evolve over time, just like yours with them. Expecting a perpetually peaceful sibling bond isn't realistic. It's entirely normal for siblings to have disagreements and misunderstandings. Instead of stepping in as a referee at every instance, guide them to resolve conflicts and talk through their differences.

As your children enter the tumultuous teenage years, prepare for changes in their sibling dynamics. The teen years are a period of self-discovery and individuation, which can create emotional distance between siblings. Stay patient and remind your teens about the value of their sibling bond. Offer guidance as needed, but trust them to navigate their changing relationship.

Above all, your role as a parent is instrumental in modeling the importance of relationships. The way you handle disagreements, show love, and offer support will significantly impact how your children relate to each other. So, let your actions mirror the values you hope to instil in your children.

Lastly, remember to take a step back once in a while and marvel at the beauty of the family you've created. Witness the authentic moments of love, joy, and connection between your children. Celebrate their unique bond and remember that you played a part in nurturing it.

The journey of parenthood is filled with shades of joy, fear, confusion, love, and much more. But amidst all, the most significant takeaway is the realization that you've created these wonderful beings who share a beautiful bond with each other, forever. That's the intensity and magic of parenting and no experience can quite measure up to it.

So, here's to the ever-evolving, unpredictable, and yet profoundly fulfilling journey of parenthood. Here's to the lessons we learn, the love we share, and the powerful bonds we foster amongst our children. Because, in the end, these bonds will be their strongest support system as they venture out into the world.

Looking Ahead: Envisioning a Future of Friendly Family Bonds

The journey of parenting, as numerous and intricate as the steps may have been so far, doesn't end with dealing with school, extracurricular activities, and modern-day challenges. Nor does it end at navigating the sensitive teenage years, or the special scenarios of blended families and twins. It is a continual growth curve, a ceaseless course towards a future where your children enjoy strong and friendly family bonds.

Envision a future where your children speak with love and respect about each other. Where they've traded rivalry and competitiveness for comradeship and support. Can you see it? That's the future we're laying the groundwork for—through every conversation, every shared family meal, every family outing, and every bedtime story.

Yes, sibling relationships will change as your children grow and their life paths diverge. They'll face challenges—high school nerves, college choices, career paths, and perhaps even global relocations. But consider this: Wherever they are, whatever they face, they'll have one thing that's increasingly rare in our swift-moving world—a deep-seated sense of belonging, an anchoring identity rooted in family love and respect.

The bonds you're nurturing now will serve as the compass guiding your children through life's complexities. The understanding they acquire through their sibling interactions will help them in handling relationships outside family circles. They'll draw strength and resilience from their family bonds, combating adversities with more resolve.

As you set the stage for lifelong friendships between your children, it's essential to remember that every child is unique and has his or her relationship rhythm. Celebrate these unique qualities and achievements. The uniqueness is not a barrier but a strength that can enrich the sibling bond over time.

Now, there will be moments when you might wonder if the values you've worked to instill are making a difference. In those moments, remember that your consistent effort is like watering a seed—it takes time to see the growth above the soil, but changes are happening beneath the surface. Water with patience, care, and regularity, and the seeds of strong family bonds will root firmly and grow steadily.

Adolescence and adulthood come with their own sets of challenges for your children—navigating burgeoning friendships, the tug-of-war of peer influence, and the fluctuating pressure of school and expectations. Yet, the skills they've honed and the bonds they've formed with their siblings will prepare them for handling these tribulations better than any school can.

Moreover, the trust and respect they've developed will not just stay within the confines of the family. They will extend to their friendships, colleagues, and future life partners, influencing their social circles positively. Think of the ripple effect—a healthy family dynamic can touch countless lives through your children's interactions with the world.

The commitment to maintain these bonds isn't relegated solely to your children either. As parents, you play a vital role in modeling healthy relationships, lending a listening ear, and providing a safe space for your children. Don't underestimate your presence in their lives, even as their worlds expand beyond the home.

When the conflicts seem overpowering, communication feels stunted, or things don't go as planned—remember the compass. You're directionally aligned towards a future of friendly family bonds. It's okay to take detours, to have days when the journey seems more challenging. It doesn't mean you've strayed from the path—it simply means you're human, and your family journey is beautifully authentic.

Looking forward, imagine the birthdays, anniversaries, and major life events. These milestones are not just individual achievements; they are family victories—testimony to the power of unity in diversity, individuality within collective identity. The shared history and future of your children are the rich color threads that weave the tapestry of a strong, supportive family bond.

The future is a landscape filled with opportunities for your children to choose love, empathy, and respect and to prioritize family amidst life's chaos. As you envision this future, remember to be gentle with yourself. Enhancing sibling relationships is a journey unfolding one day at a time.

Lastly, understand that the vision isn't about attaining a static image of perfection. It's about movement and growth. It's about two steps forward and one step back; it's about laughter and tears, successes and setbacks but above all, it's about love—love that's unconditional, patient, resilient, and forgiving. That's the truly powerful foundation for friendly family bonds and the future you're envisioning.

Appendix A: Activities to Strengthen Sibling Relationships

Activity 1: Family Game Night

One of the simplest ways to cultivate strong sibling relationships is through regular family game nights. These can be anything, from board games to card games or video games. The initiation of friendly competition and the shared experience of either victory or defeat can help to build a strong bond among siblings. It's a casual setting that lends itself to conversations, shared experiences, and camaraderie.

Activity 2: Cooking Together

Cooking is a wonderful hands-on activity where siblings can work together to prepare a meal. This kitchen collaboration fosters understanding, cooperation, and problem-solving skills. Plus, siblings have the added joy of enjoying the fruits of their labor together.

Activity 3: Book Club

Encourage your children to start a sibling book club. This activity nurtures not just their love for reading, but it's also an opportunity for thoughtful discussions and the exchange of perspectives. It encourages them to listen to and respect each other's viewpoints.

Activity 4: Collaborative Art Projects

Arts and crafts are an engaging avenue for creativity. Completing a project as a team can be a bonding experience. Siblings can learn how to play to each other's strengths and accommodate for weaknesses, working together toward a common end goal.

Activity 5: Shared Responsibility

Tasks like taking care of family pets or household chores are excellent for fostering trust and responsibility. It teaches the children to rely on each other and to share the workload, enforcing the concept that every family member is important and necessary for a harmonious home.

Activity 6: Personal Storytime

Encourage siblings to take turns telling and listening to each other's stories before bedtime. This simple activity encourages empathy and understanding and provides an intimate space for them to share their thoughts and feelings with each other.

Activity 7: Sibling Play Dates

Schedule sibling play dates which are specifically meant for the siblings to spend quality time together. During this time, encourage them to partake in activities they both enjoy. Understanding and respecting each other's interests can help break down barriers and foster a sense of camaraderie.

Activity 8: The Gratitude Game

Teach your kids the value of gratitude with a simple everyday activity. Encourage each sibling to share something they appreciate about the other. Over time, this act of positive recognition can foster a healthy and considerate relationship.

Activity 9: Family Volunteering

A great way to bond while fostering empathy and a sense of community is through volunteering. Whether it's a local food drive, a tree plantation day, or helping at a community center, these acts of service can significantly strengthen sibling relationships.

Activity 10: Create a Sibling Scrapbook

Creating a scrapbook filled with family photos, ticket stubs from outings, and other mementos can be a lovely exercise in reminiscing and sharing memories. The activity not only allows siblings to collaborate but also to appreciate their shared experiences and history.

Activity 11: Secret Handshake

Something as simple as creating a secret handshake can foster a sense of shared identity and exclusiveness between siblings. It's a small, secret bond that only the siblings share and an endearing reminder of their unique relationship.

Activity 12: Achievement Celebration

Whenever a sibling accomplishes something - no matter how small - encourage a little celebration. This simple act can help build a culture of appreciation and respect among siblings.

Activity 13: Road Trips

Taking a family road trip can be a great bonding experience. Being enclosed in a car for a long time encourages conversation, shared experiences, and the creation of unforgettable memories. It's a perfect opportunity to strengthen sibling ties.

Activity 14: regular team sports

Any team sport is a great exercise in cooperation, communication, and understanding. Being on the same team often strengthens the sense of comradeship among siblings. This also instills healthy competition while teaching the value of supporting each other for a common goal.

Activity 15: DIY Projects

Simple home DIY projects can be both educational and fun for siblings. Building a birdhouse, making home decorations, or planning a small home garden are examples. These activities can foster cooperation, division of labor, conflict resolution, and shared satisfaction in accomplishing a common goal.

Appendix B: Recommended Reading and Resources

To continue nurturing your own knowledge and skills in fostering healthy sibling relationships, it's crucial to have resources at your disposal. In this Appendix, we've compiled a list of further reading materials and websites to aid in your journey. These resources delve deeper into understanding the unique challenges and joys of siblinghood, and offer practical strategies to help you in your role as mentors for your children's relationships.

Books

1. **"Siblings Without Rivalry"** by Adele Faber and Elaine Mazlish: A guide for parents seeking to cultivate an environment at home where siblings next to live peacefully. It includes hands-on, practical advice you can use almost immediately.

2. **"The Birth Order Book"** by Dr. Kevin Leman: This enlightening book offers an intriguing perspective on the impact of birth order on personality and sibling interactions.

3. **"Peaceful Parent, Happy Siblings"** by Dr. Laura Markham: A well-known parenting expert, Dr. Markham, provides advice on how parents can promote caring, cooperative, and loving sibling relationships.

Websites

1. **Aha! Parenting:** www.ahaparenting.com. This website provides articles, advice, and parenting tips from Dr. Laura Markham.

2. **Empowering Parents:** www.empoweringparents.com. This site offers behavior management tools and tips, with a section dedicated to sibling rivalry.

3. **Sibling Relationship Lab:** www.siblingrelationshiplab.com. Run by Lynna Sutherland, this site is dedicated to exploring the dynamics of sibling relationships.

Podcasts

1. **"Sibling Relations"** by Sibling Relationship Lab: This podcast focuses exclusively on sibling interactions and offers expert advice mixed with practical applications.

2. **"ON BOYS: Real Talk about Parenting, Teaching and Reaching Tomorrow's Men"**: Although this podcast primarily focuses on raising boys, many of the topics are applicable to siblings of any gender.

3. **"Simple Families"**: This podcast often discusses sibling interactions within its broader focus on minimalist parenting and family life.

Beyond these, there are also countless online forums and social media groups dedicated to discussing sibling relationships. Be cautious, though, not all advice found in these places is necessarily sound. Apply your own judgment and intuition to discern what aligns with your family's values and situation.

Please note that while the books, websites, and podcasts mentioned above can be extremely helpful, there's no substitute for seeking professional help if needed. If your children's rivalry escalates to a point where it's disrupting your family harmony or causing undue stress, consider consulting a pediatrician, therapist, or counselor.

Also, let your children's school be a resource. Teachers, social workers, and school psychologists can often provide support or refer you to other professionals.

Remember, while this book provides a solid foundation and guidance on nurturing harmonious sibling relationships, the additional resources will allow you to continue expanding your knowledge even further. These resources should ideally be used in tandem with the principles and techniques shared within this book, not as standalone solutions. They serve as a way to add more tools to your parenting toolbox by providing a more in-depth understanding of certain issues.

Besides, your lifelong learning on this subject will also set a powerful example for your children about the value of learning, personal growth, and continuous self-improvement. So, feel free to explore and delve into these resources, keeping an open mind to the wisdom and guidance they can offer.

In conclusion, each resource listed in this Appendix is a potential treasure trove of wisdom waiting to be tapped. Use them as companions on your journey of nurturing loving, understanding, and extensively supportive sibling relationships in your home. Don't fret if some strategies or advice don't resonate; you're the expert on your family - trust yourself, trust your instincts, and always strive to keep learning.

Appendix C:
Quick Tips for Handling Common Sibling Scenarios

As we wrap up this extensive exploration of sibling relationships, let's delve into some real-life scenarios that parents often face. Although every situation, child, and family is unique, there are some general strategies that can help navigate these rough waters with grace.

1. Launching a Family Meeting

If siblings are constantly squabbling, consider having a family meeting. This is an effective tool many parents use to facilitate communication, reach agreements, or solve disagreements. Through these meetings, children learn to express themselves, listen to others, compromise, and realize that their voices matter.

2. The Favoritism Trap

Accusations of favoritism can ignite deep sibling resentment. It's crucial to make every child feel seen, heard, and valued for their unique qualities. Encourage each child's individual passions and celebrate their achievements. Remember that equal doesn't always mean identical; different children have different needs and aspirations.

3. The Older Sibling as Parent Trap

While it's natural for older siblings to help out with the younger ones, avoid casting them into parenting roles. Support the older child's independence and be respectful of their time and personal space. Show them that their role as a sibling can coexist with their own individual journey.

4. When Sibling Rivalry Turns Physical

Physical disputes should be mediated calmly but firmly. Establish a rule that violence is never an acceptable solution, emphasise the importance of respect and care for one another. Teach them alternative ways to vent their frustration.

5. Handling Shared Spaces and Belongings

Conflict can arise from sharing rooms or toys. It's essential for siblings to learn negotiation, compromise, and respect for personal space and belongings. Establishing clear rules regarding borrowing items or invading one another's spaces can prevent many misunderstandings.

6. Navigating the Minefield of Comparison

The comparison between siblings, whether from parents, friends, teachers or relatives, can breed resentment. Be mindful of this, and celebrate each of your children's unique strengths and accomplishments. Foster an environment where they feel they're valued for who they are, not in relation to their sibling.

7. Managing Jealousy and Envy

Feelings of jealousy and envy are pretty standard in sibling relationships. Open dialogues regarding these feelings can be beneficial. Encourage your children to express their feelings constructively. Teach empathy by explaining situations from the other sibling's perspective.

8. Introducing a New Sibling

Bringing a new sibling into the family is an adjustment for everyone, especially for an only child. Involve the current child or children in the preparation process. Make sure to carve out one-on-one time with each child to help alleviate feelings of displacement.

9. The Balancing Act: Solo and Shared Activities

Find a good balance between solo and shared activities. While shared activities can foster bonding time, solo activities allow children to explore their own interests and define their own identities.

10. Fostering Mutual Respect

Teach your children that everyone deserves respect, both in words and actions. Encourage them to appreciate each other's uniqueness and different stages of development, and to understand that the other's needs, likes, and dislikes might vary from their own.

11. Managing Sibling Relationships During Adolescence

Adolescence can stir up sibling dynamics, with siblings becoming more private and wanting more independence. Respect this need for space, while still maintaining family connections and communication.

12. Supporting Siblings Through Major Life Changes

Whether a family move, parental divorce, or other major transition, siblings can provide significant support for one another during challenging times. Help them understand the changes and encourage them to communicate their feelings.

13. Helping Siblings With Different Abilities

If you've got a child with specific physical, emotional, or intellectual needs, it's crucial to provide additional support for their siblings. It's essential to address their concerns, acknowledge their feelings, and provide them with the information and support they need.

14. Preparing for University or Leaving Home

When a sibling leaves home for university or work, it can be a major adjustment for those left behind. Encourage open conversations about this change, allow the remaining children to express their feelings and provide reassurance of continued family connection despite the physical distance.

Every sibling relationship is unique, with its joys and challenges. As parents, you can provide the tools, guidance, and positive role modelling your kids need to cultivate healthy sibling bonds. By navigating these common scenarios with wisdom and finesse, you're setting the stage for lifelong friendships.

Modern-Day Pressures: School, Peer Influence, and Expectations

As our children continue to grow and navigate their way through life, they are faced with increasing pressures from various sources. One of these comes from the academic environment, commonly referred to as school-related stress. School is more challenging now more than ever, and the high expectations placed on students can lead to significant pressure.

Encourage your children to approach their schooling as a journey of learning rather than a competition. Teach them that their worth is not tied to their grades, but to their value as individuals. Highlight that understanding and knowledge are more important than scores on a test. This way, they won't feel the need to compare themselves to their siblings or peers, reducing the likelihood of animosity or resentment.

Peer influence is another significant source of pressure for our children. Peers become increasingly important during adolescence, with their opinions and actions having a strong influence. The desire to fit in and be accepted can lead to unhealthy behaviors and strained sibling relationships, particularly if one child becomes a part of a group that encourages such behavior.

In these situations, it is crucial to maintain open lines of communication with your children. Assure them that it's alright to be different from their peers and it's okay not to share their friends' behaviors or opinions. Encourage your children to seek advice from trustworthy adults, including you, when they feel confused or pressured by their peers. Teaching them to think critically will also help them make well-informed decisions.

Another modern-day pressure point for our children comes from societal expectations. From a young age, children are taught that they are expected to behave in certain ways, which can create feelings of pressure. Boys may feel the need to act tough and suppress their emotions, while girls may feel pressured to be nurturing and emotionally expressive.

Have conversations with your children about these expected norms and reinforce that they should feel free to express themselves as they are. Validate their feelings and support their interests, irrespective of societal dictation. Assure them it's okay to go against societal expectations if they don't align with their true selves.

As parents, it's also crucial for us to be mindful of the expectations we place on our children. While it's natural to want the best for our children, it's important that we don't put too much pressure on them to live up to our ideals. Our role is to guide them, not to mold them into our vision of what we think they should be.

Help them set realistic and achievable goals, providing the necessary support and resources but allow them to stumble, experience failure, and learn from these experiences. It's through these challenges they learn resilience and develop a realistic view of their strengths and weaknesses.

Continue to emphasize the importance of caring, understanding, and empathy in sibling relationships amidst these modern pressures. Make it clear that siblings are not competitors but invaluable support systems for each other. Include strategies to handle these pressures in family discussions so they feel equipped to tackle them.

Promote collective problem-solving whenever a sibling is trapped in a predicament. Encourage them to brainstorm together and arrive at potential solutions. Learning to lean on each other through difficult times can further solidify their bonds.

Implement regular family meetings where everyone can speak openly about their feelings, pressures, and fears. Teach them to be receptive to each other's feelings at these times and respond with kindness and understanding. Normalize these sensitive discussions so the sibling relationship evolves beyond superficial connections to emotionally supportive and understanding ties.

Remember that each child is unique and will react to, and handle, pressures differently. Be prepared to provide individualized care based on their personalities, capabilities, and coping mechanisms. Your role is to provide an environment that encourages emotional expression and mutual understanding among your children.

Also, it's crucial to note that severe constant pressure can lead to chronic stress, which can affect a child's mental health. If you notice drastic changes in behavior, or if a child seems unusually overwhelmed, it may be time to seek help from a mental health professional.

Ultimately, teaching your children to view their siblings as allies, not rivals, can help them withstand these modern-day pressures. When they understand that they can rely on each other for support, they are better equipped to navigate through life's ups and downs.

As we wind this chapter down, it's notable to remember that the evolution of sibling relationships are affected by numerous factors, with modern day pressures playing a significant role. In our next chapter, we'll explore some strategies for adapting to changes in the family that are unique to the 21st-century.